I'll Watch From Up Here

arisi
eanna Parisi

ved.

)584

Dear reader, this book contains subject matter about abortion that may be difficult for some. As I understand this is a sensitive topic, I wanted to give you the heads up now. <3

To anyone who has ever felt an ounce of Marabelle's pain, you're not alone.

Prologue

"Jace, please, not tonight," I plead. I can feel the anger radiating off of him as he pitifully holds himself back. I step in front of him, putting a barrier between him and his potential opponent.

"Look at me, Jace," I grab his face, forcing him to look into my eyes. "It's not worth it. I'm okay. See," I keep his gaze on me.

He's pissed because, on our way out of the party, some guy was looking at me too hard. Jace said something to him, and then the guy said something to him, and they verbally went at it. The guy stalked off to the other side of the street, while one of his friends is holding him back, as I'm doing the same. We don't need this to escalate any further. I really don't feel like cleaning up his blood tonight.

Jace's face fights the words that come out of his mouth, "I'm sorry, Belle, I'm sorry. I-I- just didn't like how he looked at you."

"You don't need to be sorry. I like when you protect me, but it doesn't need to go any further than that." I tip my head over to where the other guy sits on the curb, defeated. "I think he got the hint."

I kiss him. So gently. Reassuring him that he did nothing wrong. Somehow, my touch is the only thing that can break Jace from these hazes. It happens a lot. Sometimes I'm too late, sometimes I get him just in time.

He slips his perfect hand into my back pocket. "Let's go home."

"What a pussy!" The guy from the curb yells. "You're just going to let your girl bitch you around."

He's running towards us now. "Don't start shit you can't finish," he spits.

I get between Jace and the guy like the idiot I am. But I don't even know what happens next. I know I hit the ground. I know my ass hurts. I know I got the wind knocked out of me.

Jace unleashed. Every single ounce of frustration he was holding back disappears as he pounds into this guy.

I analyze what's happening in front of me. Jace hits the guy twice, but then the friend hits Jace. HARD. Jace gets up, stumbling to his feet. The look on his face is murderous. He makes eye contact with me, and my heart sinks right before he pushes the friend to the ground.

"You hit her!" He screams. "You fucking hit a girl. My girl! What the fuck is wrong with you."

He won't stop hitting, won't stop screaming. I need to do something. I need to stop this. People from the party start coming out to see what the commotion is about. The cops will be here any minute. I know how this goes.

"Jace!" I grab his arm hard, dodging his next blow. One look at me, and he knows. He takes my hand, and we bolt.

"Are you okay? Please tell me you're okay." He takes a full evaluation of my body. "Where did he hit you, Belle? Show me where you're hurt."

"He didn't hit me, I don't think. I think he just pushed me." I want to cry seeing how he's looking at me.

"What a fucking scumbag. How could he do that?" He exhales sharply. "I could've killed him, Belle."

"I know," I brush my thumbs over his bloody cheek, "But I really don't want to love you in prison." His laugh breaks the tension.

He doesn't let me clean him up. He doesn't want me to get up.

He returns from the bathroom with a band-aid on his chin and clean wounds. I get wrapped in a nice warm blanket. "I threw it in the dryer while I washed up." He snuggles into my arms. "I know you like it this way."

Fuck. I love this boy. Even when I hate him, I love him.

The warmth of the blanket sinks into us. Wrapped limp in limp, I trace the tip of my finger up and down Jace's back.

For the first time all night, he finally relaxes into me. And I, to him.

We don't need to say anything else tonight. We just need each other.

We just needed to go home.

Act I

CHAPTER ONE

I can't seem to walk fast enough to beat this clock without burning my skin off. The coffee is overflowing in my cup—just a bit too much creamer. God, I love a sweet coffee. Sometimes, I don't brush my teeth in the morning, so I have time to make myself a proper cup of coffee. Okay, anyway, this audition starts in like 90 seconds, and I'm totally going to fuck this up if I don't get there in time. I've finally worked up the courage to audition for our school play this year.

I always thought theater kids were a bunch of nerds. I made fun of them most of my life. When you make fun of something so much, you start to realize where the root of it comes from. I was jealous. I had always wanted to be able to not give a fuck enough to sing and dance on stage. It's still cringey for me, but I try to remember how fun it was when I was a kid.

I used to sit my Mom on the couch in our living room. My Mom was home most of my life raising us. With Dad working all the time, she was able to be. She had some free time to grow her daughter's confidence and cheer her on. I have her to thank for that. She'd help me push the tables to the side of the room closest to the windows. Those enormous windows overlooked the skyline of New York City. I would grab my stereo with two purple microphones stationed on the side and let it all go. Let the music take me and perform like I had just sold out Madison Square Garden.

Being a child is so innocent. There's no judgment or fear; there's support and honor. I'm searching for that support and honor again, hoping to embrace some of my inner child this year.

"Alright, people, it's show time! Anyone auditioning for the lead, please gather to the right, and anyone auditioning for the supporting lead, please gather to the left." Mrs. Welsh is a bit benighted. That is doing me quite the favor right now. We were supposed to start at 8:30 this morning, but luckily for me, it's 8:42, and she is just beginning. She's been directing the play at Titan High for sixteen years. It's intimidating walking into this very established environment.

I rip off the sticky-soaked lid and finish my last sips of joy before heading to the left of the stage. It's tense in here. I try not to let my eyes wander around too much; I don't want anyone to think I'm nervous. Every single person in here has to have been doing this forever. There are a handful of skills in life that you have to start from a very young age to master. I am under the impression that theater is one of them.

Oh god, would if I can't do this? Would if every single person here laughs at me? I would be a joke. It's weird enough that I'm already here in the lineup. Tabitha looked like she was going to vomit when she walked in and saw me. Tabitha and I know of each other, almost everyone at my high school has gone to school together since kindergarten. It's a small town. She's basically the queen bee of musical theater. I'm basically the queen bee of parties and boys. That ain't no peanut butter and jelly. I remind myself to breathe. My mind has a habit of sprinting down a tangent. I mean, whose mind doesn't, right? Okay, just breathe, Tabitha is on the right. I am on the left. There is no sandwich-making happening; everything is good.

Each person gets called up one by one. This year's play is *Freaky Friday*, a 2000s classic. My apprehension about doing the play disappeared as soon as I heard it was *Freaky Friday*.

We're each asked what part we're auditioning for. Then, we all run through the same lines and two songs. I can't tell if we're flying through these auditions or if I'm so nervous time has escaped me. I keep noticing this boy looking over at me from the right side of the stage. I heard Tabitha call him Eli, so I guess that's his name. She seemed pretty dismissive with him, motioning him to back away from her so she could do her breathing exercises. I noticed the interaction, and he caught me catch the interaction. We smiled at each other across the stage, acknowledging her ridiculousness.

"I heard the party tonight is going to be crazy." One of the girls behind me says. "The stage crew guy, Ian, who usually throws it is graduating this year, so I don't doubt he won't go out with a bang."

"Oh, for sure, it's going to be fun. Want to go to the mall after school to get new outfits," another girl responds.

"Yes, let's do that!"

I want to turn around and get the party details but decide not to. I need to focus right now. There's only one more person in front of me.

I'm up next. Shit! I'm up next. Inhale, exhale. Fuck, that's not working. I squeeze my nail into my thigh, harder and harder, enough to break the first layer of skin. Okay, much better, that brought me back to this reality.

"Marabelle," Mrs. Welsh projects.

"Hi, that's me." I step forward out of the lineup. "I would prefer it best if you called me Belle."

I've never liked my name. When people say my name, my whole body cringes. It's like they don't say it good, or I hear it bad. Belle is best. I feel more like a Belle than a Marabelle. I haven't gotten around to legally changing my name now that I'm eighteen. It's on the list.

"Alrighty then, Miss Belle. What role will you be auditioning for?" Mrs. Welsh asks.

"Tess Coleman."

"Very well," she smiles slyly. "Let's hear it from the top."

CHAPTER TWO

I blacked out.

The entire rest of the audition. I have no idea if it was good, or bad, or anywhere in between. I head back to my car, feeling defeated. I wish I didn't do that. If I could remember how I did, I'd at least be able to gauge whether I got the part or not. I tried to linger around after to see if Mrs. Welsh would give me any indication of how it went, but she didn't. So now here I am, moping down the steps to my car.

Eli lingers at the bottom of the staircase. Considering I was the last one out of the auditorium, he must have been waiting. For me?

I'm pretty sure he and Tabitha fuck around. I mean, I don't blame her. He is incredibly sexy.

He's got that extremely tall, lanky, dead boy look about him. He resembles a vampire in the right lighting but like a sexy Damon Salvator Vampire. I'm also not entirely sure about his sexuality; he might be gay. Then again, is anyone entirely sure about their sexuality?

"Belle, hey. I was hoping you didn't sneak out the back door," he awkwardly giggles. This guy is no joke. I mean, for real, he's like super hot now that I'm looking at him up close. I knew from basic high school chit-chat that he was one of the better-looking nerds; I guess I never got close to him to notice. It's like we're conditioned to believe that the misfits have cooties. You stay in your lane, and I'll stand up on a hill and look down at you from mine. "So, uh, you were great today. I had no idea you could sing. Where have you been hiding that?"

I hesitate. "Yeah I—I usually just keep it to my shower, but I decided to step out of my comfort zone a little bit this year." I want to derail the attention off me. "Is it always that intense in there?"

"Welcome to the drama club. We've been gifted that name for a reason." He steps closer to me. I analyze the situation so fast that he doesn't even realize I've calculated the equation. I drop my eyes to scan his body. I take the final step off the stairs, standing a foot apart from him. God, he's so tall.

"Don't you and Tabitha, you know, have sex?" I will torture this boy. Make him want it, make him work for it, make him think he's going to get it, and then dispose of him. It's my specialty.

His whole face went sheepish at the word sex. "Uh, hello, I asked you a question. What are you a virgin?" I know I'm coming off aggressive, but what he wants out of this is obvious.

"Fuck no, I'm not a virgin," he spits out. "Tabitha and I have fooled around before, but she's nothing worth remembering."

Typical boy.

I stare at him all doe-eyed and pouty, exactly how they like it. I'm waiting for him to over-explain himself.

He continues, "She has wanted me since, like, second grade, and I started feeling bad for her. Like, don't get me wrong, she's not hideous, but she was never my type."

Bingo.

"She's too full of herself for me. She knows no one's a better performer than her and uses it to keep everyone else down. Not to mention she's got like no ass." Meathead. "You, on the other hand, are much more my type," he runs his hand through his stark black flow.

"Because I have a nice ass?" I say bluntly. My honesty always seems to throw people off. It's a gift and a curse. I use it for both. "Tell me, Eli, what is it about me that you find so attractive?"

"Belle, I'm not—I wasn't trying to flirt with you."

I interject, "Oh no? That's my mistake. I could've sworn that's exactly what you were trying to do."

"Okay. Maybe. But I didn't know how to ask you out. I think today is the first time you've ever really paid attention to me, and we've gone to school together since kindergarten." There's a tinge of guilt that finds a home inside me. I push it down; I stick to my formula.

I get real close to him before grazing his cheek for a moment. "I would've gone out with you, Eli, if you just asked." A total lie. "And maybe next time, don't shit talk another girl to make me feel all holy and above."

"I—I—It just." He has no idea what to say. Was I too hard on him? He pulls it together quickly, "Forget I said anything." His hand reaches out to shake mine. "Friends."

I guess he's not so bad, and as long as he's not actively trying to fuck me, I could probably use a theater friend. I sigh loud enough for him to hear, "Friends, it is." We shake hands to acknowledge our union.

Giggles erupt from both of us. Probably from embarrassment, partially from awkwardness; nevertheless, we laugh and let the moments escape us. We're both standing in the exact same spot with the exact same expression on our faces, not really knowing where to go from here. I decide to break up this awkward tension.

I'm good at this. I know what to say when no one else does. I've been doing it for most of my life. I start, "I heard some people talk about a party tonight, are you going to that." This is my in. I didn't hear much from the two girls behind me, just that one of the stage crew guys, Ian, was throwing a party, that it's tradition after audition day. I don't know when or where, and considering that this is a new social circle, I have no access to that information. I figured why not use Eli a bit to find out."Do any of you guys even drink?" I add.

Eli starts walking to the parking lot, so I follow his lead. He looks at me, "Of course, we drink, Belle. Do you think only the popular kids have fun?" His tone is gentle when he continues, "The theater nerds, as you may call them, can drink," he says with extra emphasis on the 'k.' "Sometimes too much. We've had a couple scandals with kids having to get their stomachs pumped."

"A couple? Jesus."

"Yeah, I know. For the most part, our parties are super fun. If you throw a bunch of actors together with some alcohol, there's bound to be some drama."

We approach my car. I wonder how he knew the red Chevy was mine. Maybe people know more about me than I like to admit. He's large enough that his arm rests on my car like it was made for him. "How about I pick you up at 10 tonight, and you can really see what we're all about."

"If I agree, this isn't a date." I want to make that crystal clear.

A smirk forms on Eli's face, "Not a date. A proper initiation for you. You're going to get the part, so better get acquainted with these people." He points at me and wiggles his finger around, "Just an F.Y.I. princess; you're a theater nerd now, too."

There is no frustration in my tone when I say, "See you at 10. I'll meet you at the corner of Madison and Palm." I brush past him and hop in the driver's seat. We both smile at each other as I drive home.

CHAPTER THREE

Inhale. Sharp exhale. I know he's here before I even walk through the door. I saw his Mustang on the street as soon as I opened my car door. There was a spotlight on it. I couldn't miss it.

I called things off with my on-again, off-again, situation ship, boy thing with Jace last night. I'm tired of his shit. We've been going back and forth for almost two years now. I let the whole label thing go for a while, but now that he's in college, it's hard to ignore. It's too weird for me. Dating a college boy was great for my reputation and all, but now that I have to compete with college girls, it's not fun.

Insecurity isn't something I'm too familiar with, but it consumes me when it comes to Jace. Him going to college has just heightened that. He comes home Thursday to Sunday to see me. It's not sweet, it's calculated. I want to be able to focus on this play and finally let go of him this year. I thought I did that, but now, here he is, at my house.

I wouldn't doubt that my mom was the one to let him in. She loves Jace, thinks he's good for me. If my mom took one second to realize I've been screaming for help, she wouldn't have opened her arms so easily to him. I grab my door handle, close my eyes for a moment, and enter.

As soon as I walk in, no one in my family is anywhere to be found. I guess I couldn't assume that my mom or sister would be home because I didn't check the garage to see if her car was there. Great. So it's me and him.

I scan the living room, but he's not here; he's in my room, waiting for me. I stomp up all my stairs and then a ladder. I live in the attic. I petitioned to about four years ago; it was my only way of escape. I couldn't share a room with my little sister forever. Besides, Lindsay and I are six years apart. When I started high school, I wanted no part of sharing a room with my eight-year-old sister.

As I open the door, he's the first thing I see, sitting at the edge of my bed. My bong in one hand, and flowers resting on his knee. Sunflowers, my favorite.

Jace stands immediately, seamlessly placing my bong on the floor while simultaneously picking up the flowers. Somehow, everything he does is smooth. The boy never misses a beat, perfectly refined. Almost like he was created by a god or a machine. He opens his mouth, "Belle, I don't like how we left things between us."

Is he shitting me? That's what comes out of his mouth first. He continues, "Where were you all day I have been waiting for you since 10 this morning."

I roll my eyes and don't move.

He sets the flowers down next to the bong, romantic. "You're not going to come here?" He opens his arms for me. "Come on, baby. I don't want to fight."

It took all of three seconds, but I'm pissed now. My blood is boiling. I raise my voice, "All we do is fight, Jace. I'm tired of it. You can't just come into my house without permission, bring me flowers, baby me, and expect everything to be fine." I inhale another gasp of anger, "I told you last night there is no us anymore; I am done for real this time. I want to be my own person."

I can see something change behind his eyes. Jace launches off the bed closer to me so we're face to face.

He knows this one will hurt, but he wants to make sure it will sting. "Cut the shit, Belle. Stop trying to be someone you're not. Whatever the fuck this is about is temporary. You can't just change overnight," I can feel his breath ricochet off my face. "You need me, Belle, and I—" there's a slight hesitation, "I need you. We're the same. No one's going to put up with you like I do." He cups my face with both his hands. Twisted. I close my eyes.

Do not cry. Do not cry. Do not cry.

I can feel the warmth of his hands absorb my pain. The smell of him like a familiar hug. He is my home, and I am a lost cause without him. I don't know who I am without him. He lifts my head and forces me to look up at him. "Do you love me?" He asks.

"Yes," I whisper.

Jace returns to regular speaking volume, "Then nothing else matters." He kisses me then, hard and desperate. There's passion and fire, and all I need right now is this moment. Nothing else matters. I need him. I need to feel him deeper. I replicate his despair. I know he has to leave soon. He always leaves on Sunday nights. Is it so wrong to have him for a little? Can't I just have this moment?

Jace breaks my heart over and over, but he's the only one who's been able to put it back together.

I break the kiss. Pushing him onto the bed, I climb on top of his lap. I don't say anything, crisscrossing my arms to pull off my top. I let the black v-neck flop to the floor. He knows what's coming. This is what we do. We fall apart and come back together. We hit each other where it hurts and tenderly sew the wound in a jagged stitch.

I am nothing but a rag doll, and him, my seamstress.

"I love you, Jace, and nothing else matters. I'm sorry I tried to push you away. It's just been hard while you're at school. I feel guilty that you come home so much to see me," I take a breath. "I'm worried I'm holding you back from the full college experience." A lie. I want him to come home less so I can put my full effort into this play. I don't want him to not come home at all. To be honest, I would miss him too much, and nobody fucks me like he does.

As he unhooks my bra, he says, "Baby, please don't worry about that. I'm actually going to be helping at the student center to tutor people. I'll have to spend a lot more time on campus. The three-hour drive here will be a lot to do every week." He runs his calloused hands up my back.

My breath hitches in my throat; he's distracting me from why he really came here. "How often will I see you?"

"Often enough," and he takes me in again. Jace is always so cryptic. He never answers questions directly. It's always innuendos and arrogance out of his mouth. God, he infuriates me. I know well enough not to question him further. He's getting impatient. He picks me up and flips me under him.

I beg, "Fuck me, please."

CHAPTER FOUR

I wonder if I totally botched that audition. It couldn't have been that bad. Eli said with such confidence that I'm going to get the part. I try to review the exact words he spoke. Did he say I will get the part, or did he say he hopes I get the part?

The cold water flashes on my skin and snaps me back into real life. I've been in this shower for well over fifteen minutes. I guess I'm running out of hot water.

I gear the knob of the faucet as hot as it will go. No, no, I think Eli said the part is mine, so now I'm a theater nerd. Why can't I remember exactly what he said? It was something along those lines. Maybe if I wasn't so busy guessing his next move, I could recall his words verbatim. My mind races through the scenes of this morning, trying to find comfort somewhere. The speaker cues up the next song; I need to stop. I have to get ready. I'm on edge. I'm anxious about this party later, anxious about the audition, and anxious that I may have driven Jace away for good.

I exit the shower and find comfort in the blue fuzzy mat under my feet.

Eli should be here in roughly an hour, and I have no idea what is appropriate to wear to a drama club party on a Sunday night. I'll admit I'm a little nervous to be getting wasted on a Sunday when I have school tomorrow. I can't believe these theater nerds don't care. Seriously, I have to stop calling them theater nerds. If I get this role, I'll be one too, and I can't have that title floating around about me.

I throw on my usual party attire—wide-leg green cargo pants and my favorite crop top with a big peace sign on the chest. I decide to add a black zip-up. Maybe I should lay low this party; these aren't my people.

"Knock, knock, knock, we're home, Belle's," my little sister shouts from the bottom of the ladder. "Can I come up?"

"Yeah, come on up and tell me if this outfit is cute." I hear my Mom whisper something to my sister, but I can't quite make it out. The ladder creeks loud enough for me to expect the two of them to arrive.

My Mom looks tired. Somehow, through her exhaustion, she always manages to keep that sparkle in her eyes. I'm not sure where they went today, but Dad didn't come back with them, so I wonder if it has something to do with that. Sometimes, he stays at his friend's house. It's a very much don't ask, don't tell kind of situation.

My Mom takes a seat on my floor, bringing her knees into her chest. She looks me up and down and asks, "Miss Belle's, what are you getting ready for at 9:30 on a Sunday? You know I don't mind you going out on a school night, but this doesn't look like you're going to hang out with your friends," she motions to my outfit.

I don't hesitate, "There's a party for all the theater kids tonight. It's some post-audition tradition that they do. I feel like I have to go to get acquainted with everybody."

A head nod of approval from my Mom. "Hmm, I see. How did that go today? Do you think you got the part?"

Lindsay comes to sit on the dresser beside me. "Of course she did, Mom. Belle sings like an angel," she adds with an extreme amount of sass. "And she's the biggest drama queen I know."

Turning to face Lindsay, I smile genuinely and say, "Thank you."

Lindsay is one of the few people who bring me true serenity in this world. She was the main reason why I wanted to audition. We were constantly doing skits together and making up choreography growing up. My Mom blessed both of us with unwavering confidence, and we love showing it off. Lindsay told me I should audition for the play a couple of months ago. When I heard Mrs. Welsh wanted to re-create the play version of Freaky Friday, it felt too right. That's one of my favorite movies. And so I figured if I'm going to do it, I should go big, which is why I auditioned for the role of Tess Coleman, the supporting lead.

My Mom is in my closet now. Clearly, she doesn't approve of my outfit. "Hey, sweetie, if this is supposed to be a first impression, maybe you should wear something a little more showbiz."

"Ew, Mom, that doesn't even make sense," I regret the harsh words as soon as I say them, but I won't ever admit that. I grab the new shirt she's holding in her hand. "This?" It's a sheer black top. I almost forgot about that shirt. My Mom is the most gorgeous woman in the world, so I no longer feel the need to retaliate. I lean over to kiss her on the cheek, "I'll change, thanks." And that's my way of apologizing.

A car horn goes off three times fast. I guess that's Eli.

As we're driving to the party I can feel my nerves start to increase. I was fine when I first got in the car, but now that the music is blasting, I can barely hear myself think. Eli mentioned before that we're not picking anyone else up. I thought that might be his tactical approach, but he's not doing any of that weird, flirty stuff right now. I'm actually starting to feel like he could be a real friend.

I hit my bong before I left. Once—okay, maybe twice. I shouldn't have hit it twice. The first hit, I didn't think, got me high enough. I don't really plan on drinking too much tonight, so I figured one more hit for my sobriety and nerves wouldn't hurt. It's hurting.

We pull up to a gorgeous red brick home. Cars line the entire street, clearly indicating there's a party going on. Eli shifts the car into park while lowering the stereo. He stops the ignition and reaches behind me, grabbing a bottle of liquor. He tips the nozzle to me, winks, and says, "Shall we?"

I tap my fist to meet his cheers, "We shall."

It's funny because I do this thing where I just kind of turn on and turn off. It's so beyond subconscious that my body knows exactly when my mind needs the switch. Right now, I'm turned on. Everyone's face is a hue of liquor and guilt. How much alcohol do we have to drink to feel something?

How much weed did I have to smoke to not feel anything?

I can't afford to go down this rabbit hole of teenage angst. These people already have made assumptions about me. If I'm really going to be co-lead in that play, I need to prove myself. Upon countless introductions I've tagged along with from Eli, I'm starting to make my way back into reality. I need alcohol to counteract my highness.

Approaching the kitchen, Eli grabs my arm, "Shot clock?" He says.

"You read my damn mind. Yes!" I'm relieved he can sense my discomfort. One shot down the hatch, at least it's vodka. People start to join us; it's always easy to rally people to do group shots. It's strength in numbers. Everyone who's standing around the counter I don't know by name, but I recognize their faces from today. We all nonchalantly acknowledge one another and proceed to shove burning liquor down our throats in unison.

I slam my glass down to the counter after five shots. "Anyone want to play a game or something?"

The petite blonde girl giggles, saying, "The games are just about to begin."

The music cuts and everyone's attention already knows where to go. I follow their lead. "My fellow people of theater, it is with great honor that we are here for another year to celebrate audition day." This must be Ian. He has the most delicate curls atop his head. I must not have noticed him today because he's a part of the stage crew. He's standing on the corner of his sofa. We're all huddled around him. He continues, "The games will begin in the next 60 seconds. I will explain the rules, and then the timer will begin."

I look up to Eli, confused, "Is this serious?"

"I think you're going to like it," he responds, dead serious.

Ian raises his voice, "The rules go as follows. One, the party continues as normal. Anyone who appears to actively be looking for the impostor will be escorted from the party." He pauses to point to the seven people standing beside him. "These lovely fellas will kindly or forcibly remove you. Two, no outward alliances can be formed. Three, betrayal is encouraged; the better you deceive, the better chance you have at winning." Everyone seems to be excited about that. Ian's finger placement mimics the following number, "Four, you have until midnight to catch the impostor and turn them into me. If you turn in the wrong impostor, you will also be asked to leave. As this is my last and final year before graduating, I am offering you all a hint."

I'm still confused about what this game even is. I'm hoping this hint will clear things up. He steps down from the couch, "Checkered," he speaks lightly. Quickly raising his glass into the air he screams, "Cheers to *Freaky Friday* which will be our best show to date, and cheers to the impostor!"

The entire room lifts in an uproar. What the fuck is happening. After those shots, I'm not sure I'm in the same reality anymore.

Everyone seems to have returned to business as usual, as if that entire speech had never happened. Huh?

"I'm gonna go take a piss," Eli says.

"Wait, what the fuck was that? How are we going to find the im—"

Eli clasps his hand over my mouth, pinning me to the wall behind me. I had no idea he was so forceful. He stares at me deeply, "Shut your mouth, or we're both going to get thrown out of this place." There's something so serious behind his actions. "Getting thrown out is a thorough hazing process. I don't think you want to be a part of that. Listen to the rules and find the impostor." His grip over my mouth drops in an instant. Did that turn me on?

I push off the wall, meeting his gaze. "Don't ever touch me like that again." I stalk off in the opposite direction. I have no idea what's going on. From what I've pieced together, we're all supposed to party normally, even though there is an impostor among us that we're all trying to find. We can't talk about what's going on to form alliances. Oh, and if we get thrown out, it's not just a bye-bye go home you suck, no, you get hazed. I do not underestimate these drama kid's hazing tactics either. It seems like they're all taking this game very seriously, so I don't doubt that they haze the fuck out of you.

What kind of fucking party is this?

CHAPTER FIVE

It's been like— I don't know how long because I'm drunk. I've been drinking and dancing, trying to fly under the radar. About half the party's population is gone. Eli is still here. I haven't spoken to him since his aggressive, sexy, pin-me-to-the-wall thing. He's been running the pong table pretty much this entire time.

    I haven't looked for this impostor person, not really. There was a girl in a checkered top that I danced with for a little, but I thought it was too easy of a target. She was escorted out about 30 seconds ago. It's like the goddamn *Hunger Games* in here. People are reluctant to go, and the house's energy is getting increasingly cutthroat. A couple of people thought I was the impostor. I suppose that's fair, I even started to believe it at some point. Is the impostor even aware of their imposting? I don't know; Ian didn't make that very clear in his rules. I'm over this. I want to smoke and go to bed.

I've poked around the house but smell no weed. I make the obvious choice to go outside. Two dudes are making out on the right side of the deck, but still no weed. This cool air feels too good to go back inside. I also don't want to interrupt this romance so I keep walking to the left into the yard. Three boys exit a small shed and tip-toe to the property line. They come up to a chest-high fence, hop it, and run. That was sketchy. The shed has a slight hue of light illuminating the window. Those kids were definitely smoking in there. I'm going in.

Tearing open the door, I see three buckets and a makeshift couch made of wood. Some kid is squatting on one of the buckets, rolling a blunt. He's using the other in front of him as his rolling table. He doesn't glance up at me immediately. My presence doesn't even startle him.

"Sup," he finally says, looking up from work.

I'm skeptical, but I know my priorities. "Can I join you?" He motions his hand for me to sit down on the wooden couch, so I do. "I'm Belle, by the way," I say awkwardly.

He licks the backwood, drawing it towards him with his full lips. "Your name is Belle? No, it's not, tell me your real name."

I counter, "That is my real name, I prefer to go by Belle."

He counters, "Well, that's contradicting. What you prefer to go by isn't your real name." He makes his final seal on the blunt and places it between his two fingers, grabbing a lime green lighter.

There's something about this boy that I like. Maybe it's just refreshing to step out of that godforsaken party, but this is much better.

"My name is Nicholas, but you can call me Nick," his hand is out to shake mine.

"Marabelle." We shake hands not making full contact with the blunt and the lighter blocking us.

He's smiling for the first time, "Much better, I like that."

We pass the blunt back and forth in silence. I'm feeling much more sober now, this is exactly

what I needed. I've shaken that awkwardness. Not to mention, this is a well-rolled blunt.
But no one rolls like Jace.

"So, what part did you audition for today?" I say.

The smoke is trapped in his lungs; he's laughing uncontrollably, trying to fight for some oxygen to enter his body. "I don't do the play, Marabelle. That's much more my brother's thing."

I take the blunt from him, "Who's your brother?"

"Ian."

"Ian is your brother!" I exclaim.

"Is that so surprising?"

I think about it for a minute. Ian is thin and pale and looks nothing like Nick. Nick is strong and has rich, tanned skin like mine. Hmm, his skin is almost exactly like mine. He must be hispanic because no regular white person is this tan in the middle of the winter.

Nick smiles, "We're stepbrothers, and I'm messing with you. My Mom married his dad when we were in 7th grade. I don't mind Ian, though; we're cool."

I laugh, feeling embarrassed, "Stepbrothers, right."

"Hey, can I get the lighter this went out?" He reaches for it, but I'm pretty far away. Instead, he scooches to the other bucket he was rolling on earlier and grabs the lighter from me.

I glance down at his hands in the exchange. They're perfectly manicured hands. Rough yet soft. Unique for a man. He takes care of himself. Something about his hands strikes a cord in me. Perfectly manicured hands with clear polish on them. Perfectly manicured hands, with clear polish on them, and one checkered pinky nail. One checkered pinky nail. "Oh fuck," I exclaim out loud. "You're the impostor."

He leans into me, grazing my thigh with his arm as he puts the blunt out in the tray beside me. He slumps right back into his original position. He's not smiling anymore. " You got me, Marabelle. Now you have to turn me in." I can't help but think this is a trap. How did I not notice before?

I'm cautious with my words, "I don't care about that stupid game. I literally just wanted to get out of there and smoke." I exhale loudly, "It's almost twelve. I'm going home as soon as all this shit is over."

He gazes at me with deep longing, "You know the winner gets first dips on their dressing room. The drama kids are always complaining about how dingy those rooms are, there's only one renovated space." This is starting to make much more sense to me. "Don't you want the room?"

I lean forward, realizing how fucked up I am. All those shots are starting to really sink into my bloodstream, I can feel them affecting me. For the first time all night, my anxiety has subsided. I grab his hand, grazing my thumb over his pinky nail, "I don't want the room. But I like your nails."

Standing to leave, I can feel the energy shift in the room. He doesn't want me to go. Maybe he wants me to turn him in.

He stands, too. "It's refreshing to see someone like you auditioning for the play."

Does he know me?

"Everyone knows you, Marabelle; it's hard not to be aware of your presence."

Nicholas wants me. Welcome to the club. I know how that sounds, but it gets a little redundant when every guy pulls out all of their best tricks to try and get in your pants. They just want to see if it's true. If I'm as good in bed as everyone talks about. I can act like a whore, I can prance around and make out with too many people to count, but no one can have all of me. Some can enter me, and I can get them off, but no one will ever penetrate my heart like Jace.

His hazel eyes glow from what I can see in this hazy shed. He's handsome. Typically too muscular for me, but I don't mind the space he takes up when he's next to me. Fuck. That's it. Tonight sucked. I found the impostor; the only reward-able thing to do is kiss him a little bit, right?

I sit back down looking up at him with desperation. "How aware are you of my presence now, Nick?" My hand reaches to the back of his thigh. I gently grab on prying him towards me slightly. His black cargos are distressed beyond belief. It looks like he's fallen on pavement several times in these things.

When a girl is presented before you with your crotch in her face and desperation in her eyes, there's really only one thing to do.

Nick cups my cheek, toying with one brown curl dangling from my face. He's looking at my lips when he says, "When was the last time someone pleased you?"

I'm shocked, my face twitches back in resistance. He holds me in place. I inhale air to retaliate with words, but he stops me. His thumb brushes the swell on my bottom lip.

Our eyes are locked.

"When you're ready to stop letting these boys treat you like shit, let me know." His right-hand snakes its way around my neck, up the back of my spine, to the crown of my head. He has a handful of my curls.

I am covered in chills.

Nick takes hold of my hair, pulling just enough. A hushed moan escapes my lips. "God, you're so fucking beautiful." He pulls my head up to look at him in the eyes again, "The things I'm going to do to you."

I feel caged. I feel completely out of control. But I somehow feel safe and seen for the first time in my life. A pounding on the door breaks our connection.

Ian shouts, "Alright, Nick. It's 12:05, and nobody got you. I'm going to head to bed. I'll see you tomorrow."

Nick smirks. Without opening the door, he responds, "A bunch of idiots, let's clean up in the morning."

"Yup. Thanks for volunteering, man. Lunch is on me tomorrow. Night."

And we're alone again. Nick speaks first. "I'll be seeing you again, Marabelle. Get home safe."

I don't know why, but the words form before I can even stop them, "I look forward to seeing you, Nick. Goodnight, impostor."

CHAPTER SIX

Monday morning is a drag. It's third period now, and I barely remember getting myself together for school this morning. I saw a couple of the theater kids through the halls. We shared mutual glances of knowing as we passed by each other.

I dump my history exam on Mr. Nelson's desk. I finished in thirty minutes so I have a spare thirty of free time. My choices are free time on the computer or resting my head on my desk.

I choose to place my head on the cushion of my arm and close my eyes. I know exactly where I'm going to go, the crevice in my mind that stores my Jace memories. I miss him and haven't heard from him since he left. I can't help but feel like yesterday was some sadistic form of a goodbye. I want him out of my life. I want to be free from the chokehold he has over me. This time, it feels too real. Like he might be pulling away from me. What's that thing cynical people always say? Careful what you wish for. Yeah. I get it now.

I don't like where my mind has spiraled. It's time to change the script. That boy last night, he was—I don't know. Different. Any other boy I've ever interacted with would've accepted the make-out and the mind-blowing blowjob.

I was done with the night. I just wanted to feel something. I think I've been trying to feel something for a long time. I thought he wanted the same. They always do. It was the way he spoke to me. The way he cupped my face like I was so incredibly delicate. I am incredibly delicate. *When I'm ready to stop letting these boys treat me like shit*, huh, who does he think he is. He was cute. He was dominating. I could toy with him a little.

The bell blares through our ancient speakers, and the ruckus of the room infiltrates. I pack my things. I'm starving.

"I heard little Miss confused by the game was the one who found the impostor," Eli's behind me in the bagel line.

"You're talking to me again?" He must think I forgot about his little outburst.

"I was never not talking to you, Belle." He reaches for the cream cheese. "I'm sorry about that, by the way. Sometimes I take things too far."

You think? I grab the butter. "It's fine, Eli," I wink, "It kind of turned me on."

In truth, it was pretty terrifying. A part of him lost control, and I don't like that. I'm not a problematic girl, though, so I accept the apology. He's still the only friend I have in the drama club.

Laughing through words, he says, "Postings will be up after school. See you then?"

Oh shit, I find out today if I got the part. "See you after school."

I didn't realize how consuming this play stuff is going to be. I take an audible exhale and plop down at our usual table by the windows in the back. My whole friend group has already made their way to their seats. Brandon is usually too high because he always spends most of our lunch asleep or in the cookie line. Kelly and Madison are arguing with Joey about the new *Barbie* movie. He very clearly doesn't understand that Barbie was so much more than a plastic doll with big tits.

Elena squeezes my arm in greeting; she's much more affectionate than I am. It's one of the things I love most about my best friend. She swigs a sip of my apple juice and clicks her tongue, "So I heard through the grapevine of Titan High School that you tried out for this year's Spring musical."

I'm not that caught off guard. Elena is the FBI agent of our school. She keeps tabs on all one thousand-two hundred students. I know she's not mad.

"Yeah, I want to do something different to close out high school. We graduate soon, and I thought it was time to sing somewhere that wasn't just my shower or in the car with you." I slide her the rest of my juice. "Is it nerdy?"

Elena gives me a crooked smile. "It's a little nerdy Belle's, but what the fuck do high school kids know about what's cool and what's not." She smiles, "We all just follow a social hierarchy because boxes keep things clean. Do the fucking play. You were born to blur the lines."

"I find out today if I got the part," I shrug. "I'll call you tonight with the details."

"And Jace?" Elena knows everything that went down between Jace and me. Every separation and every reunion. Sometimes, she gets frustrated with me and my undying love for him, but she's always there to support me however I need.

I toss my refinements of lunch into the trash. "He came by yesterday with some bullshit I love you, let's not fight." I laugh hysterically, "He brought flowers, Elena. Flowers!"

"He's getting desperate." She laughs. "He has never done that."

Maybe he is getting desperate, maybe he cares more about me than I thought.

"So, is this really it?" She's eyeing me, praying for a real yes.

"I don't know. We fucked, but the whole thing felt like a big goodbye. He said he's going to be tutoring on campus this semester, so he won't be home as much."

"He sucks."

"Yeah, so that's a loose end." But it doesn't have to be. "Hey. I thought you'd be the best person to ask. What do you know about Nicholas Ricci?"

Her eyes widened. "Belle, why are you asking about the most mysterious man at this school?"

"I was acquainted with him last night. He's—he's captivating."

"Now, this I love for you. I feel like he's into some freaky sex shit. He's got a darkness to him." He appears that way, but I felt really light in his company.

Elena continues, "All I know about him is that he trains at a private MMA gym. "

"No wonder why he looked like he was chiseled by a god," I say grinning.

"I'll see what I can find on him."

I grab her arm harder than I want to, panic flooding into my gut: "Do not let it get back to him that I was digging."

Elena looks me in the eyes, "Relax, Belle, I'll keep it low."

The rest of my day is anything but school-related. My mind is still occupied by the events that transpired last night. Also, if I got the part.

I'm obsessing about my interaction with Nick, and I can't shake it. I want to talk to him again. I didn't give him my full charm. I was so caught off guard that my guard wasn't anywhere to be found. My guard never goes down. I can't afford it. Nicholas Ricci, MMA guy; I like him. I want him to like me.

CHAPTER SEVEN
Jace

"I'm out of here. See you guys tomorrow!" I grab my flannel, toss it over my shoulder, and head out of the student center. I've been on campus for six hours today. Three hours in class, three hours tutoring idiots how to pass their class. I haven't stopped thinking about Belle. I want to reach out to her and see if she's doing okay. I had to make Sunday a goodbye. I couldn't exactly say that because I didn't need her whole performance, but being at college has been too hard on me. I can't be caught up in thinking about where she is or what she's doing. Without me in range, I feel completely useless. Belle and I can't be trusted apart. I tried to make it work; I damn near drove myself insane driving back home every weekend to go see her. I miss her like hell, but I know she'll be there when I come back; she always is.

I was on autopilot the whole walk back to the dorms. The next thing I know, my hand is wrapped around my bong, and my mind is shut off. I like myself better when I can't hear myself think.

After three hours of playing Xbox, my thoughts creep back in. I never gave a definitive we're together or we're not. That means she could be doing things with other guys, but it's Belle; she wouldn't. I went there because I couldn't stand how she ended things with me. She doesn't have the power to do that. I love her too much to not fight for us. But then, right before I stuck my dick in her sweet pussy, I confessed that I won't be home as much because I'm tutoring. Which is true; I am tutoring, and I need the extra cash since tuition went up second semester. I guess I went over there so I could be the one to end things. I had to make amends to have her again, one last time, because would if when I come home again she's finally smart enough to not want me.

I should text her to see how she is, if she misses me.
Me: I bet you're smiling reading this text.

No answer. It's been over an hour, I haven't heard back. That's so unlike her.

My breath grows shallow. Fuck, I'm so high. I hope my roommate Oliver doesn't come back from the dining hall yet. I can't be around people when I'm this high; I start to get panicky.

My phone sounds off. There she is.

Belle: Close to a smile, why haven't I heard from you?
Me: Because I've been waiting to hear from you.
Belle: I thought Sunday was your covert way of saying goodbye?
Me: It's not goodbye I'm busy at school now, I don't know how often I'm going to be home.

Why can't I just say it, just tell her that it is goodbye, and we're both better off apart for now? I keep typing. If she's not going to do it, I will.

Me: I don't like being apart from you. I think it's best if we go our separate ways.
Belle: At least for once, you were able to say

**what you're really thinking. Good luck with
the rest of school, Jace. I love you, always.**

I love you too, Belle's, always. Is what I want to say, but don't. It's better to let her go.

I'm surprised that she didn't put up much of a fight. That's better. That way, I didn't have to put that much of my energy into going back and forth and possibly changing my mind. I should go out tonight. That would help. The beauty of college is that there's something to do every night. So, for the people who are lonely and searching to divulge their souls into something that's no good for them, college is the perfect place to be. I need to hook up with someone else. Truthfully, I've had my eye on a couple of girls but haven't acted on it much. I don't like the idea of being tied down, especially not with Belle. It would be too permanent for me, too real. Maybe one day, but I want to live my life now and be settled down later.

The door clinks open, "Jacey boy, why you got that grin on your face?" Oliver places a Styrofoam box down on his desk.

"We're going out tonight, Oliver. I need to make out with a bunch of women." And forget about Belle.

He reaches for my hand to dap me up. Slapping my back, he says, "Yes, bro. It's time for you to start experiencing college to the fullest. That girl will be there when you get home."

I like Oliver. The first semester, I had no complaints, and the second semester has been off to a great start. He's a massive dick, a tremendous player. He's the kind of guy who believes he can have multiple women at a time but would never like one of his women to reciprocate. He pulls it off well; somehow, none of them ever know about each other. It's like he's living in the 1800's. He's got a finesse about him I envy. He's way more comfortable with his sexuality than I will ever admit.

"I'm gonna jump in the shower; let's start pre-gaming in 20."

CHAPTER EIGHT
Marabelle

Shut up. Shut up. Shut up. I can't listen to anyone else say a single fucking word. I'm about to explode. I can feel it coming. Jace texted me last night that it's officially over. Now, it's tonight, and I'm just starting to feel the weight of it. All last night I was fine, happy even. Today at school, fantastic. We had our first rehearsal today for *Freaky Friday*. I got the part, minimal celebration.

I saw Jace texted me shortly after finding out the news. I was about to tell him, hoping he would be open to hearing. Instead, he had other ideas. Ideas that involve him leaving me.

"Belle's you still haven't told us anything about rehearsal?" My sister has been nagging me for details since I walked through the door.

"It was good," I say coldly. I shift my energy towards my Mom. "Can I be excused? I have a history project due tomorrow and haven't started." My Mom doesn't care about my made-up history project or the fact that I haven't started it. What she does care about is her granting permission for me to be excused. It's always about respect when it comes to my dear mother.

Mom grins, "You may be excused. We're leaving in 30 because Lindsay has dance at 7."

Good, I'll be alone for a couple of hours. I need to be alone. "Okay," I say, pushing away from the dinner table.

It takes me forty-seven steps to get from the dinner table to my room. It takes forty-seven steps to feel my throat overflow with molten hot tears. It takes forty-seven steps before it's safe to release them. Painfully, I sink into myself, collapsing against the back of my door. Bringing my knees into my chest, I rest my head as low as it will go. There's no reason to keep my head held high.

I should quit the play. I should call Jace. Maybe I should call Eli because he would pick up. I'm not good enough to be the supporting lead. Why the fuck is the world doing this to me? I feel empty, I feel broken, I feel like nothing could make me feel worse than Jace does. Yet, all I want is for him to hold him.

My eyes slow to a close, heavy from all the tears falling. I'll never forget that day we had together this past summer. He had come home from a Yankee game with his dad. While he was there, he texted me that he wanted to see me after, couldn't wait to see me after. When I got to his house, his entire room was dark and cold; that's always how he preferred it. He groaned for me to come crawl in bed with him. Jace was drunk; he was cracking up, explaining to me that his dad was able to slip him some drinks, and by number five, he was feeling it. We didn't fuck right away that day. We laughed and rolled around in each other's arms. He loved to play fight with me. I think he liked to see me a little mad. I think something about it turned him on. Breathless and dumb, he laid over me, caressing my face, tracing the lines of my lips. "I love the sound of your voice," he told me. "I love your lips and the way you kiss me." I didn't know what to do. Compliment after compliment, he was pouring into me. He never did that. It was the second time he dropped his walls. And the first time, he let me have a glimpse into his internal monologue. His monologue for me. I basked in it. Let it drown me. I didn't know how long it would last. I didn't know if I would ever get it again. "I really love you, Belle, and I'm always going to love you."

"Bye, Belle's, see you later," Lindsay screams from downstairs.

BANG. The door shuts, and they're gone. I can't feel the memory anymore. It's faded away into the abyss of our love. I'm back in my room against my door. My cheeks are stiff from my fallen tears. I take my phone and whip it as had as I can onto my bed. That felt good. I need to throw something else. My history textbook goes next. I don't need to break anything cause I'm already broken. I need to feel the release of this edge.

He's gone. Did I ever need him? Breath heavy, I crawl to my bed. I will not let him have this kind of control over me. He never brought much good into my life anyway. One in twenty-five good memories. Those are bad statistics. He's at college fucking a million other girls with perfect lips and sexy voices. I don't care about him. At least no one can know that I am dying without my other half.

Wetness falls to my thigh.

That's the last tear I drop tonight.

"You have five seconds to get in my car before I come inside to kick your ass," Elena shouts through my phone speaker. I completely forgot she was picking me up to hang out at Brandon's.

I hang up before I say anything, grabbing my hoodie and running out the door. Flopping my hood over my head, she gives me a look. "I'm fine. Please don't ask me what's wrong. Put something good on. I want to sing and get high."

"Got it. Singing in the car with bestie playlist is going on now."

Going to Brandon's is routine business. This is where we all come to smoke. Brandon's parents don't care, considering they're huge potheads, too, so it works out for us. Everyone's here tonight; me, Elena, Kelly, Madison, Joey, and obviously Brandon. We assume our usual spots around the couch, pass around a couple of joints, and stop what we no longer want to feel. Giggles and smiles are our only worry now.

Elena's legs are draped over mine at the L of the couch. Once everyone is lost in the show on the TV, she switches her attention to me. "I did my digging, and I believe you'll be pleased."

"You mean about Nick?" I sit up straighter.

"Yeah, I didn't want to tell you in the car because you were all emo." I suppose I was. "So, apparently, he's in our grade, which I never knew. He isn't the biggest social butterfly and has no known friend group at our school. A reliable source told me that some of the other kids from the neighboring town train at his MMA studio, and he's really close with them."

That was probably those three boys I saw escaping the shed. They all had a similar build to Nick. "Anything else?"

Elena reaches for my phone. She has an evil smile on her face. I love when she's devious. A few clicks later, she opens her mouth again, "I found his Instagram and his ex-girlfriends."

"You sexy little bitch," I slap her thigh resting on me, "This is why I love you." Yanking the phone from her hand, we begin our stalk. I would argue this is the most fun part about talking to a new guy.

Although, Nicholas Ricci doesn't have much to offer us. He has three photos up. One of him and his Mom when he was a baby. Another of him and those three boys, it looks like they just got done fighting in a sweaty dark gym. The last is a selfie, unusual for a boy. No boy is ever confident enough these days to post a selfie. They think it's "gay" or something. Little do they know that's all the girls want to see. He looks sexy. He has a black beanie and an oversized hood over top of that. The lighting is just perfect enough to capture the hazel in his eyes and the swell of his lips. It's crazy how fast my gears change.

"He's hot."

"I agree," Elena switches profiles, "and this is his ex."

She's pretty. Brunette. Very fair skin, cute pink cheeks. She's the opposite of me.

I guess he doesn't have much of a type. I was never one to put other women down, so if she's in his past, that's where she belongs. A strong voice whispers into my thoughts, *Jace is in your past and then in your present, on a loop. Would if that's how she is for Nick?* That's very insecure of my brain.

"From what I've gathered, his ex moved to Florida. It seems amicable. She shouldn't be anything to worry about."

I am beyond grateful for Elena sometimes.

CHAPTER NINE

I'm finally adjusted to my new schedule. Going straight from an eight-hour school day to play practice was tough at first. I was so used to napping after school that I was yawning the whole rehearsal for the first two weeks. Playing Tess Coleman is slowly becoming second nature. I'm so supported by my fellow theater nerds that I am even considering myself one. In between scenes, we get to fuck around. It's nice.

I've seriously gotten to know Eli from spending so much time with him. We've been carpooling to school together every day. He's not into me. He's into anything with a pulse. The kid is extremely horny, which naturally leads to his flirtatiousness. On our drive home from rehearsal yesterday, he confessed to me that he's a virgin. I was shocked. I assumed we were getting close, but I didn't know we were getting to the point in our friendship where we shared our darkest secrets with each other. He told me it's his biggest secret that he feels really embarrassed by it. I liked that he trusted me. I can keep a secret.

He explained to me that every time he's almost gotten there with a girl, he gets too nervous and stops himself. He's done everything else, but when it comes to actual sex, he freezes up. I asked about Tabitha because it's a well-known thing at our school. He said she would give him head a lot and that he wanted to take it further but couldn't. So, eventually, Tabitha gave up.

It was really nice to be able to talk to a guy so openly about his performance anxiety. Typically, I would've made fun of him and thought it was pathetic, but in the context of the situation, compassion was the best route.

The play kids are breaking my exterior. I'm not mad about it. They have such a deep sense of self. I'm learning that you have to in order to switch in and out of character successfully.

My scenes are done today, and Tabitha will be operating her solo scenes for the rest of our time. While backstage, getting ahead on my homework, I realized I had left my notebook in my locker. I whisper to Eli that I'd be right back if he could watch my backpack for me. He gives me a head nod, and I step out.

How did I forget to take my notebook? It's the only thing I need for my homework. Which is due tomorrow. I must've been rushing to get to rehearsal. My mental checklist usually never lets me slip up, so I'll have to make note of that.

Big, bold, captivating energy consumes me. I feel someone's presence step beside me.

A deep, sultry tone I recognize. "Marabelle?" Something I couldn't forget.

Nicholas.

I turn it on. Glimmer and lust flood my face as I open my body to him. "Nicholas. I was wondering when I was going to see you again." This guy fucked with my head the last time I saw him. I was drunk and confused by some freaky party rules. He might've caught me off guard again this time, but I'm prepared.

"Me too, but you know my offer."

Pushing my locker closed I stand taller, "I almost forgot your little offer. Now, I remember. Lucky for you, I'm ready to accept." What I'm ready for is to shove my tongue in his mouth.

Effortlessly, he says, "Then come with me when your rehearsal's over."

"Like right now? You want me to leave with you from here?" He's got me flustered, "How'd you know I'm in rehearsal? And what are you even doing at school this late?" It's not like he plays a sport here. Maybe he's a creep.

Nick takes two steps in just close enough to tease me. "So many questions Marabelle. I had detention for consecutive tardiness. I was on my way out when I saw you." Without hesitation, he continues, "I don't want any drama. I'll be in the parking lot closest to the library waiting for you if you want to join me. I won't wait forever."

I weigh my options. Well, really, this is my only option, and it's doable. Eli drove me to school today and was going to drive me home, so I don't have a car here. Also, our rehearsal will be done in about fifteen minutes. Most importantly, I owe nothing to Jace. Sometimes, when Jace and I are off, I feel a sense of guilt, a need to remain loyal. This time, though, it's different.

"I'll see you in 15." I was grinning when I said that, and I'm grinning my entire walk back to the theater. Something about that boy dissolves my calculations.

"That's a wrap for today," Mrs. Welsh announces as I walk back in. Have a gorgeous weekend, my loves. We will pick up where we left off on Monday."

Grabbing my backpack, I look up to Eli and say, "Hey, Eli, I'm good on the ride home today."

Mr. Sarcastic responds, "Oh yeah? Are you planning on flying home?"

"No idiot," I smack the back of his head, "Ian's brother is going to take me."

"From the way you're eyeing me, I take it you want me to keep this hush-hush."

I glare, "Yes, Eli."

He brings me in for a quick hug. "Well, be careful. I don't know much about Nick."

"I don't think anyone does."

"I always knew you were a little freak. Bye, Belle, I can't wait to hear how this goes."

I wink and begin speed walking to the library exit. Is this going to be a make-out in his car kind of hangout, or is he taking me back to his place? He knows I like to smoke. Maybe we're going to do that. Uh-Oh. I really hope we don't smoke. I'll be way too anxious to have a casual smoke sesh with him. Reaching for my phone, I text Elena really quickly.

Going to hang out with Nicholas Ricci (: Call you later! xoxo

I can spot Nick standing next to his car through the glass doors. He spots me immediately. There's a hint of relief that coats his body. Was he afraid I was going to blow him off? I take note of that. He's got to have a weakness. All humans have weaknesses. I have to figure out what his are. He can never figure out what mine are.

"So where are we going?" I say, getting into the car.

Our doors close in unison. "We're going to fight."

CHAPTER TEN

We pull up to some dingy back alley parking garage. This boy could totally kill me. Of course, the thought has crossed my mind. Anytime a girl is alone with a guy, the first couple of times, that thought crosses her mind. At least, it crosses mine. The car shifts into park, and he reaches behind my head to the back seat. I flinch in response, not realizing what he was doing.

Taking hold of a red duffle bag, he places it on his lap. Concern fills his eyes, "So jumpy." He grins. "Let's go."

I follow his lead up to a black door. It's covered with stickers, some worn and ragged and some fresh, all with the same logo: *MMA Studio*

1, with a red fist coming up through the center. No way, this is where he took me.

Nick pushes through the door, and the hum of the overhead lights buzzes through the space.

"What are we doing here, Nick?" I ask.

"This is where I train. No one will be here until 6:30." He motions to the space around us, "We have the whole place to ourselves."

"You want to hook up with me in some ratty old gym?"

He flings his bag off his shoulder. It hits the floor with a loud thud. Before I can blink, he's in my face. "I didn't take you here to hook up with you. That's not my intention at all." Gripping my face, he speaks through his teeth, "You're much more special than a hookup. I want you to start seeing that for yourself." He releases, "They keep spare clothes in the girl's locker room. Change. And meet me out here."

I obey. I do not want to defy him.

My options are booty shorts: sports bra or leggings: sports bra. Well, if we're not hooking up, then I don't need my ass cheeks hanging out. I put on the leggings and the sports bra. They had several sizes, all in fresh packaging. They must get a lot of people who pop in for the day. I go to stand in front of a massive eight-foot mirror. Looking over my shoulder, I decide I'm taking these leggings home. They are just the right amount of compression in all the right places. I didn't need the booty shorts, my ass is popping anyway.

But it's not about that. It's not about how good my body looks. He said I am special.

Rounding the corner of the girl's locker room I see him start to tape up his hands. He must've changed too because he's barefoot, no shirt, and has athletic shorts on. I drink in each and every groove of his body. I've never been with a man with this much grit. Jace gets into a lot of fights. I'm constantly cleaning up his cuts or begging him not to start anything when we're out. It terrifies me. It enthralls him. This is different. This is a controlled environment. This is not Jace.

Nick changed much quicker than I did, he probably wasn't checking out his ass in the mirror.

"So we're going to start very basic today. You can wear these," he says, handing me sparing gloves. "This is where I come to let my anger out." Nick pauses, "Healthily."

"How is this healthy?" I ask.

Maybe this could be healthy for Jace.

"Practicing MMA allows me to funnel my energy into something good. I used to be very outwardly aggressive when my Mom and Dad got divorced." He lays the last piece of tape over his wrist. "My Dad put me into classes when I was eight. I've been competing ever since."

He's being vulnerable with me. I don't know what to do with this feeling. "So why am I here?" Defensively, I continue, "You think I'm some angry girl who needs to punch things to feel better?"

He holds my hands, placing each one in the gloves carefully. "No, Marabelle. I think you're misunderstood, and it eats away at you. You might also have some fun. If that's so hard to believe."

He shows me some basic punches, blocks, and kicks. He demonstrates with the air each time and then has me replicate it. He hasn't hit me once. I don't know why I thought he was going to. This man is sexy. Primal. Every time I throw a punch or a kick, it brings me back into the present moment. My brain has a habit of switching in and out of reality. Fantasy land with primal Nicholas is hot, but that's not reality. Jagged breath, slick skin, and a pink glow beginning to travel to the surface of my cheeks is my current reality.

"You're picking this up a lot quicker than I thought. You're strong."

His words are validating in a convoluted way.

"This is fun. I can see what you're talking about now." I want to express the vulnerability I neglected before. "I have all these thoughts that are coming up, but as soon as I make contact with your mitts, I'm right back in the present moment."

He smiles, "Yeah, exactly. No matter how crowded your head can get, the impact will always snap you out of it. Just wait until you start getting hit. That will definitely snap you back into reality."

He sensed a shift in me, so he elaborates, "I would never hit you. Boys do not fight girls here, and vice versa. But regardless of that rule, I would never."

Glancing down at the floor and then quickly back up to him, I nod once, understanding.

"You want a water break, or you want to move on to grappling?"

"If that's the one where we get to be on top of each other, then let's do that."

He laughs, shaking his head, "Get on the ground before I put you there."

Inching closer, I open my dumb mouth again, "Mmm, please do."

In one swift motion, his hands are under my thighs, my legs are wrapped around his waist, and I'm placed on the ground beneath him. God, he's quick.

Nick puts his hands on either side of me, trapping me in his center. "This would normally be the part where I kiss you," he teases.

"And why won't you, Nick? I know you want to kiss me." Fuck. Do I want to kiss him?

"Because kissing you would be our end game." He pushes off the mat, standing up on his knees.

I pick right now to ask what has been on my mind for weeks. "Why do you think boys treat me like shit?"

Climbing up he sits next to me, close. I guess I changed the mood so I sit up too. "I've heard a lot about you, boys talk. Everyone talks about how seductive and attractive you are." He chews on the corner of his lip, "If you want me to be really candid, they say you go around." He uses air quotes, "that you're "for the boys," which is gross. I don't like when guys talk about girls that way. Not to pull the I'm different card, but I can't help but feel like you are, too. "

I open my mouth to speak, but no words come out.

He continues, "The last two years of school, you're the main topic of conversation. It didn't take long for me to notice who Belle was. I didn't see a girl who gave a good blow job; I saw a girl who was misunderstood. Because what I wasn't hearing from these guys is that you have sex with them. And most importantly, I wasn't hearing that you give your heart to them." He shrugs, "I could be reading into things, I don't know. I saw you let your guard down at the party with me, and I liked who I saw."

I'm speechless. My mask has been on so long that I forget I put it there. He can see right through it. Sometimes, I wonder if anyone has caught on to me. To the facade, to my bullshit. I respect him for his problem-solving skills. Who the fuck is this boy?

I unstrap my gloves and place my hand over his. His nails have changed since the night of the impostor game. He's got one yellow smiley face on his ring finger now. I run my thumb over it. "I'm choosing to trust you right now." I take a long blink. Inhale. Exhale. I open my eyes, "I can't describe it, but I like who I am around you. I feel safe and seen. I didn't know what it was, but you see right through my bullshit."

Nodding, Nick says, "Yup. I want to know the real Marabelle. If you're willing to keep showing her to me, I'll reciprocate."

"I'm willing to try." We clasp hands in union, and I use his strength to bring myself onto his lap. Straddling him, I get to explore his face. My thumbs roam up and down his soft cheeks. He sinks into me, relaxing his sharp jaw.

"God, do I want to fucking kiss you, Marabelle." Nick's eyes slow to a close.

I bring my forehead to his, "Can I ?"

"Not today."

Part of me is hurt, and another part feels respected. We stay frozen here for a long while.

CHAPTER ELEVEN

Nick dropped me off at home a little while ago. I went straight into the shower. I needed to wash all this sweat off of me. That, and my dirty thoughts that have lingered their way into my home. I don't even know what just happened between us. Today was a good day. I enjoyed fighting with him. I liked feeling strong. I probably haven't laughed like that in a while.

On the drive home, he mentioned that the studio does open gyms once a week. I told him I wanted to start going. He said that today was his day off, and depending on the day, sometimes he's there and sometimes he's not. The thing is, I don't need him to be there. For once, this isn't some grand master plan to get a boy to like me.

To infiltrate his space, take up his brain waves, and manipulate him into thinking I am the best option. I know I could destroy Nick. I don't want to.

I do want to start sparring more. Growing up, I was never made to feel strong or encouraged to join physical sports. For some reason, young girls are less empowered to explore physically. I liked that Nick didn't make me feel like I was some dainty girl. He spoke to me with direction and confidence. I felt like his equal.

I know I don't need another thing added to my plate. However, it is the second half of my senior year, and my workload is nearly nothing. I've already applied to all the colleges I wanted to. My only priority from now until my graduation in June is the play. And now, letting my aggression out in a healthy way. I didn't realize how much I had stored in there until today.

Jace could benefit from finding healthy ways to release his anger. He would be pissed if he saw me today. Jace aggravates me. Jace is the breaking point to all my aggression.

I cannot believe he is still making his way into my head after a day like today. I have a good guy in front of me, an amazing guy, so what am I doing circling my thoughts back to that asshole.

Jace was in the back of my mind today. He's always somewhere in there. I didn't think I was doing anything wrong, but it's hard not to compare the two. Jace would've never acted the way Nick did today. He would've fucked me the second I gave him the eyes. Nick didn't even let me kiss him for fucks sake.

My phone starts buzzing. Message after message, our friend group chat is blowing up. I finish packing my bong and grab my phone. It's nonstop. Madison mentions something about her parents not being home this weekend. Brandon keeps sending random GIFs.

DING DING DING. I can't scroll up fast enough to see what's really going on.

I FaceTime Elena. The sinister ringing continues as I rip the bong. Exhaling a cloud of smoke right into the camera as Elena says, "I'm coming over to get ready at your house, I have nothing to wear!"

I clear my throat in a half cough, "Get ready for what?"

"Madison is throwing a party. Didn't you read the chat she—"

I cut her off because what I have to say is way more important, "No I didn't read the chat, I've been recovering from my afternoon with Nicholas Ricci."

Her hand slaps over her mouth, "Oh my God, that's right! I'm coming over. I need to know everything."

Seventeen minutes later, Elena is creaking her way up the ladder to my room. Throwing her backpack onto my floor, she b-lines for the bong. Her hands grip the familiar glass, and she gestures, waving her hands dramatically around me. "Okay, I can't take it anymore. Please tell me what the fuck happened today."

I waste no time. I tell Elena every single detail of today. I always tell Elena every single detail. She's someone I can trust, perhaps the only person I do trust. I get all the way up to the part after our heart-to-heart. "I am on top of this man, forehead to forehead, on some intimate ass shit."

Her jaw has been dropped this whole time.

I continue, "I asked to kiss him. At this point, I wasn't even all juiced up on his sexiness; I literally was feeling something happen between us. I just wanted to be closer to him."

"Marabelle, you're making it sound like you didn't kiss!" She screams.

"We didn't!" I smash my head into my pillow. "And I liked it!"

"This boy plays a good game."

I get defensive but keep my tone playful, "That's the thing though, this isn't a game for him. He really likes me. He doesn't want any of my bullshit. He wants me."

"Damn. So this is the real deal, like marry him type shit." She smiles, "You really liked that boxing stuff?"

"It's mixed martial arts," I correct, "and yes, it was empowering."

"Oh, I like this," Elena exclaims. "What a fucking day, Belle. The real question is how do we get him to the party tonight."

"I don't think I want him coming to Madison's. Party me is quite the opposite of authentic me."

Laughing, Elena says, "Exactly, it'll be good practice for you."

"I guess I could text him and see if he's even around."

"Yeah, text him. It is Friday, he might already have plans." I do want to see him again, so I throw it out there.

Me: Hey, my friend Madison is throwing a party tonight. IDK if you're free, but if you are, I would love to see you there.

He responds immediately.

Nick: Hello Marabelle. I heard about that. My friends and I are going to stop by around 11.
Me: I'll see you later then, Nicholas.

Elena has begun to remove everything she shoved into her backpack. I know she'll start raiding my closet soon. She holds up a very tiny top, "So, how slutty are we dressing tonight?"

"Nick said him and his friends heard about the party and are planning on coming at 11."

She claps her hands together, "So slutty." We both laugh simultaneously. Tonight is going to be fun.

We've been getting ready for over an hour now. Mostly singing and dancing around my room with a side of getting ready. Lindsay joined us at some point, she always loves to hang out when the girls are getting ready. There's something so pure about being a little sister while you're big sister and her friends get ready together.

Elena wants her hair pin straight, and since Lindsay is better at it than I am, she's doing it. Twelve-year-old girls nowadays are like professional beauty gurus, it's mental. Lindsay has a whole arsenal of Sephora products that she's using on Elena. Her hair is looking fantastic. The girl knows what she's doing.

I decided against my standard party attire tonight. Every time I get dressed, I usually have boys in mind. The male gaze is the only reason I do things the way I do. The way I drop my eyes when I'm talking to them. The subtle touches that aren't too much, but just enough to get their body hot. The exact way I strategically pick out school outfits revolved around when I will get up during class to use the bathroom so they can see my whole body. It's all of those little things. I remember getting dressed in middle school and constantly wanting my butt to show. Whether that meant tying my shirt or pulling it up, to me, it meant sexy, which meant I was being validated by the male species. I still need that validation. I almost don't know who I really am or how I really flirt because it has all been shaped around what I think a guy will find attractive. Nick doesn't want me to seek his validation.

    Standing in front of my mirror, I observe what I've put on my body. These jeans are baggier than what I would go for; the shape of my butt isn't as prominent. I've layered a leather vest over a fitted white tee. Definitely not what most teenage girls are wearing to a party. This is my style, though. A little baggy, a little edgy, and a whole lot of me. I finally lock eyes with myself in the mirror. My hair is on point today. That is one thing I never changed about myself, my big giant curls. In my case, boys liked it, and I wasn't willing to change what made me feel the most connected to my culture.

Lindsay's squeaky voice breaks my thoughts, "Marabelle, you look pretty. Please don't change."

My sister has always had x-ray vision into my insecurities. "I won't." I roll my eyes at her. "Elena, your hair looks perfect. Linds, you did such a good job. For the play, you'll have to do mine like that."

Elena chimes in, "I just need a little lip gloss, and then we can start drinking."

As my sister claps the iron around Elena's last strip of hair, I let her know, "All right, sista , time for you to leave the big girls alone."

Elena reaches into her backpack to dig for lip gloss when she remarks, "Ah, Belle, when was the last time you talked to Jace?"

"Like a couple of weeks ago, why?"

"Cause I'm watching him pull in front of your house."

"Ha ha, very funny. Now do you want to mix with Gatorade or—"

I'm cut off by my phone buzzing on my desk. We all go silent, exchanging glances with each other. Even Lindsay looks uneasy.

"Bro, what the fuck is wrong with him." I vent.

I guess Elena wasn't joking at all.

Lindsay grabs my phone and double-clicks the side button, ending the incessant buzzing. "Here," she drops my phone into my hand. "I don't think he's worth your time anymore, Belle's." She exits my room.

Here he goes again, looping me right back into his charade. I need to answer his next call. Yes, there will be another, and another, and another. and if I don't answer, he'll come inside anyway.

Elena's still peeking through the window. "Please don't let him ruin tonight."

Everyone can feel my energy shift when he's near. How can everyone else notice it except for me? My phone buzzes again. It only passes three times before I pick up. "Hey Jace, what's up?"

"I had a free night. I thought I'd come up to see you," he says as if he's not right outside my house!

"Oh. Um, I'm actually not free, so tonight wouldn't work for me."

His gentle tone changes, something only I can decipher. "What do you have some little high school party you can't miss?" Always making me small. "It's only 9. Let me just see you before you have to go."

I look over to Elena. My eyes are pleading for approval. It's not even that I need her permission. It's that I don't know how to withhold my own. She mouths to me, *I can meet you there.*

She can meet me there, it's not that big of a deal. People don't start showing up until eleven, anyway. We were going to go around 9:30 so we could help Madison set up. The pre-pregame, and then the pregame. Or if you're from Jersey, it's the shirt before the shirt.

I take an audible exhale. "Since you're already outside of my house, Jace, you can come in until I have to go."

CHAPTER TWELVE

Elena and Jace will cross each other in passing. There's no way around it. She's trying to get all her stuff packed before he walks up those stairs. She's been around Jace like a million times. I think as of our most recent ending, things feel different, for everyone. To be fair, Elena hasn't heard me talk about anyone else except Jace for the last two years. There have been one-off hookups here and there but nobody worth remembering. I've been talking about Nick. I've been excited about Nick. I can't help but feel that Elena's relieved to see me attempt to escape my constant loop.

The sharp sound of her zipper jolts my thoughts. "Belle, you better show face later. I don't care if you fuck him. I don't care if you guys have to cry in each other's arms, but you better get it out of your system before 11 o'clock tonight."

"I know," I whisper. "A huge part of me wants to say fuck all of you and cry myself to sleep alone." I swig the vodka bottle.

Bringing me in for a hug, Elena says, "If you can't leave for you, then remind yourself that Nick will be waiting. He doesn't go to our parties ever, so obviously, he's coming for you."

One final squeeze, and I can feel him. I could throw up wondering if he caught any part of that.

"See you in a little Belle." She taps Jace on the chest, giving him a face. "Always a pleasure." Elena has been giving Jace that face since they first met. Her: I want to stab you, but my best friend loves you face.

"See you later," I nod in agreement.

Jace is looking me up and down. Similar to how I scanned my own body in the mirror before. We see myself the same. He comes to me, grabbing hold of my waist. There are layers of fabric he has to get through before he can feel my cinch. "This is new for you, I like it."

But I know he hates it. It's one of the many ways he gives me empty compliments. If he really liked it, he wouldn't be pulling it flush to my skin for my figure to reveal itself to him.

I go over to sit on the bed, "Why didn't you tell me you were coming? I don't like when you show up like this. You said we were done."

"I know what I said, Belle," he joins me. " My mom's birthday is tomorrow, so I came up to celebrate with her. My workload was light this weekend. I couldn't drive home without passing your house. And then I realized I couldn't drive past your house without calling. Can't we just enjoy each other when I'm here?"

"I don't know Jace. I've been okay without you," and that hurts me to say. "I'm scared if I enjoy you," I pause, "Even a second of you, it will take longer for me to be okay when you leave."

He puts his head down, shaking it from left to right, "I shouldn't have come. You're just," a pause, "my home. It didn't feel right not coming home. I've been struggling without you. I can't eat. I can't sleep."

He's giving me a touch of vulnerability. Sometimes, he does this when he knows I'm being kind of serious and sticking my ground. He does look pretty skinny. I can see it in his cheeks.

He stands coming to look at the dried flowers next to my bed. "You kept them. It's been almost a month, and you kept them." He crushes some of the dried petals between his fingers. The yellow dust descending onto my nightstand. "Tell me I should go, Belle, and I won't come back."

"I couldn't get rid of them," I shrug. I'm getting weaker. Every reason he's not good for me becomes farther and farther away. I reach to sweep the remnants of my dead flowers when he takes my hand. He brings me up to face him.

Silently, we're frozen. His arctic blue eyes locked on mine. It was one of the first things that drew me to him. When I saw tears shed from those eyes. They were pleading and desperate. That was the night I fell in love with him. He felt safe enough in my presence to confide in me, even fall apart in front of me.

That was the only time he'd ever done that. Looking into his eyes now, I want to scream my agony away. I wish I could forget the way he makes me feel; insufferable disposition. We're a mirror to one another. He grabs me at the same time I do. Our lips connect, and we morph into each other. He's passionate with his affection. It's a kiss that has no end. We were brought together by the god of temptation, and *god* does it feel good.

Jace breaks the kiss first, "Lay down," he says, "let me taste you."

Ripping off my jeans, I watch him watch me. He tilts his head in disapproval.

"What?"

"Your top, too." He demands.

I do what he says. I'm completely bare for him. He yanks my legs open, spreading my flesh. He wastes no time before he's on my clit. Sucking hard, my legs begin to shake from the hypersensitivity. He loves it. Every time he moans on my pussy, it sends me into waves of pleasure. I love that he loves this. It doesn't take long before it becomes unbearable. I speed up my breaths to mimic an orgasm.

Running my fingers through his hair, I tug on it gently. "Come here," I instruct. "I want to fuck you."

Something behind his eyes has changed. He's completely feral. Jace climbs on top of me, dick hard, white undershirt still on. I ruffle under the fabric to find his soft skin. He rarely takes his shirt off. I'm always reaching under to feel his skin, to feel closer to him.

He bites my lip, and I moan into him. It feels so good to be close to him again. Burying his face in my neck he picks up the pace. He gives me all he's got before he's cumming onto my stomach.

After we've cleaned up, we lay there for a while. Wrapped limb by limb in each other's arms. We don't say much. I scratch his back in lazy circles over and over again. He was right, he is my home. This is my home.

It's got to be about 11:30 by now. I thought about the party once since we finished fucking. I want to go because I don't want to disappoint Elena. Another part of me knows that this moment with Jace is temporary, and Nick could be permanent. I can't be thinking about Nick. That's bad. What the fuck is wrong with me.

Finally, Jace sits up. "Can I hit your bong?"

"Of course, there should be weed in my grinder." Now's the time to check my phone and see how much damage I've done. Elena has texted me twelve times and called four. Good thing I put it on Do Not Disturb before Jace came inside. Her last text says:

Nick is asking where you are !!!! What should I tell him???

Shit. That was fifteen minutes ago, I wonder what Elena told him. Hopefully, not that I'm fucking my ex and marinating in his body heat.

I take my phone off of Do Not Disturb and text her back that I'm still going to try and come.

"Jace, you want water? I'm gonna pee and grab a water."

"Yes, please."

Up the stairs back to my room, I'm trying to figure out how to cut our night short. I don't know if I want it to be cut short. We're getting along so well. He knows I have to leave, but obviously, he won't bring it up unless I do.

Oh no. Fuck. Jace has my phone in his hand. "Who the fuck is Nick Belle?"

Oh fuck. "I-um-what do you mean who the fuck is—"

He squeezes my phone so hard it actually might pop. "Nick, Belle. Who apparently called twice. Oh, and then he texted you asking why you're nowhere to be found."

"Jace, relax. He's a theater friend," half true. "I have no interest in him like that," is completely untrue.

"Shut up. How about you just shut the fuck up for once." He throws my phone on the ground. "I guess this is why you've been okay without me. You found a new toy to fuck you," he spits.

My gentle approach is out the door. This means war. "I haven't fucked anyone since you left me. I haven't even kissed anyone." Inhale, "Why the fuck are you looking at my phone anyway? Do you have no trust in me?"

"Don't pull that shit with me. I know you better than you know yourself. I didn't go through your phone. It wouldn't stop fucking buzzing. I thought I could glance over at my—" he hesitates. "I thought I could glance at your phone without seeing another dude's name."

"My, what, Jace? What were you going to say? What even am I to you because I'm sure as hell not your girlfriend, and I'm never going to be your girlfriend. You've made that crystal clear."

"Marabelle, do not fucking brings this back to that right now."

I know exactly what he's talking about. "Bring it back to what Jace?"

"The fucking labels." He shakes his hands out in front of his chest like he wants to strangle me.

There he is. The boy who undeniably disappoints me every time. I can't breathe. I can't do it again. What the fuck is wrong with me.

All of his clothes are on now.

All of my tears are under tight restraint.

"I think it's best if you go."

"No shit Belle."

"Why do you have to be such a dick all the time?"

"It's who I am. It's who you love. Do us both a favor and stop loving me," and with that, he's gone.

The door slams. I can let myself cry. It's my fault. I should've never let him in. You don't treat the people you love like that. He's never wanted to officially make me his girlfriend. He's inferred that's what we are, hinted to it, but he's never asked me. After the first year, I asked, you know, just wanted to make sure we were dating. That was our first big fight. It has been the root of all our fights. He doesn't feel the need to "put a label on us." I wish he felt a need.

I keep holding on tight to the bits of love he chooses to give me.

Elena's calling again. "Hello, " I answer.

The noise of the party is consuming. She screams over it, "I can't hear you, but you can definitely hear me. If you're picking up, that means he's gone, and whether you're crying or smiling, I need you to get to Madison's so we can drink it off."

"I'll be there in 5," I shout.

I'm already tipsy stepping out of the Uber. I've been chugging a Gatorade bottle full of vodka the entire drive. I almost texted Nick back, but figured I could give him a better apology in person.

My anxiety is on ten. The more alcohol I consume, the more I'm praying for this feeling to subside. I don't want to talk to anyone. I don't want to do anything.

I don't want to fucking be here anymore.

Being alone right now is not an option, so I keep walking up the back driveway.

The party is still pretty jumpin'. It's almost midnight, which usually means peak party time. The first person I see before I even step foot inside the house is Nick. Of course. He looks like he's leaving. He's pushed through the crowd all the way to the back door. His usual posse follows closely behind. His enclosed figure leaves the comfort of the glass door and presents itself to me.

"Marabelle," Nick says surprised.

"Hey, are you leaving?" I tip my head back to say what's up to his friends behind him. "I'm sorry about tonight. I had something come up and —"

He steps closer to me to keep this more private. "It's alright. This isn't our normal scene, so we're going to head out." He looks me in the eyes, "I only came to see you."

"Well, I'm here now," I force a smile. "One round of pong, and then you can decide if you forgive me."

"I forgive you, but I respected you more than to stand me up," he explains.

My calculations are off. I can't charm him. I can't seduce him. I can't fucking do anything. Maybe if I could ease my anxiety long enough to get my game back, I wouldn't be fucking this up so bad. All I can see is Jace telling me to shut the fuck up. I should just shut the fuck up.

Nick continues, "You seem distracted anyway. We're gonna go." He moves to the side of me, "Have a good night, get home safe."

Why is he keeping this so brief?

There's no point in fighting this. I've been defeated. "You too, Nick," I reply. And just like that, another one is gone. I'm going to puke. I shove more vodka down my throat.

The rest of the night is a downward spiral into my solitude. I'm there, but I'm not there. I can hear the hum of the music echoing in my head, but I don't care to dance. I talk to my friends like I'm on autopilot. Elena knew as soon as she saw me not to ask. She knows she'll get the details when I'm ready. The party is fun from what my physical body can remember. My spirit has no recollection of ever being there. It doesn't rejoin my body until I pour myself a cup of coffee the following day.

CHAPTER THIRTEEN

"We're all booked for our annual family getaway!" My mother announces to all of us standing in the kitchen. For once, my Dad is here. It feels like I only see him every so often nowadays. My mother has this perpetual need to get the family together every year for Easter. We usually rent a cabin house somewhere in the woods. It's a fun trip because of the mandatory attendance so we all get a chance to regroup and bond together.

In our everyday lives, the bonding only occurs between my sister, Mom, and me. I think that's why this weekend is always so crucial. We get our Dad's undivided attention. It's nice to remember he isn't just a father but our Dad. That weekend always reminds all three of us how much we love him and how good of a Dad he can be when he isn't working all the time or spending time with his friends.

It's too bad I'm not going this year. None of us have ever missed it. I have other mandatory obligations I cannot blow off. "Yeah, Mom, about that." I trail off sucking in air between my teeth.

"Oh no no no Marabelle. It's only two days. That is all I ask of your time," she says calmly. "Whatever party is going on will have to wait. There will be others."

"Mom, I wouldn't miss Easter for some party; who do you think I am?"

She responds, "I'm not sure these days. You've been going out more often than usual and coming home messy. You know I don't mind that you drink, but you're pushing it too far."

So I've been out like a couple of times since Madison's party, big whoop. I've been doing double sessions on the weekends. One night with the theater kids and one night with my usual group. Half hoping to possibly see Nick again. Half hoping to forget my existence. I haven't seen Nick in school. I haven't heard from Jace. Not that I want to, just pointing it out. I went to open gym the last two weeks at his MMA studio but didn't see him there either. I have been enjoying it, though. The weekly lesson helps me get to Friday, then the weekend takes over, and I'm washed into a wave of intoxication.

I defend my honor, "I'm wondering why it took you this long to say something Mom. If it's been so concerning for you."

My Dad decides to use his voice. "Marabelle, you need to speak to your mother with respect."

Raising her hand to my Dad, my Mom says, "Mateo, please stay out of this."

I laugh because he has to be joking, thinking that he has no control over how I speak to my Mom. Now I'm annoyed."This is unnecessary. I'm missing Easter because I have a mandatory play rehearsal. I can't miss it. Not sure if you guys pay attention or not, but I have a pretty big role."

"There's no way you can talk to your teacher?" My Mom reasons, "It is a holiday weekend why would they schedule a rehearsal on a Holiday weekend?"

"It's a Christian holiday Mom, the whole world isn't Christian." Of course, she doesn't understand that.

"Well, if you're going to miss it, then I'm going to be really disappointed in you." My Mom crosses her arms.

I open my hands, shrugging my shoulders, "Then be disappointed in me."

Lord, do I love petty disagreements with my family.

This day needs to end, and I'm just about ready to end it. I lay my head to rest.

Making *Freaky Friday* a musical is hysterical because it was not written as a musical. I'm honestly impressed with Mrs. Welsh's work rewriting the script. She's made the transition seamless. It's fun to break out in song right after Tess and Ana switch bodies. Tabitha and I may not be the best of friends, but she's a phenomenal lead. This girl was born for theater, so I've been taking lots of pointers from her.

"And five, six, seven, eight, go one, two, three, four, go five, six, seven, eight," Mrs. Welsh snaps along to her count. "That's it, Marabelle. Really feel the words!"

I've been working on this number nonstop, trying to get it right. It's the final scene of the play. The song we're singing is *Don't Want to Grow Up*. We took it straight from the movie. I just don't want to be here anymore, I don't want to be doing this. I have this feeling inside me that is anticipating my shatter. I'm so close, so so close to the edge. I have scuffs and scratches coating the inside of my existence. One final nudge, and that will be it.

I want to get out, take me away.

"And that's a wrap for today!" Mrs. Welsh says. "Great work, everyone. This play is coming together beautifully." She waves her hand to me, "Let's all give Miss Marabelle a round of applause for doing an extra good job today."

The room breaks out in applause. I'm embarrassed. I don't like praise. I don't deserve it. I know what she's doing.

Eli prances over, clapping in my face.

I laugh, throwing his hands to the side. "Yeah, yeah, I'm amazing," I click my tongue, "It's nothing new. "

"You want to come over later a couple of us are going to run some lines," he smirks, "as in drink some beer and not run many lines."

"Ah, I would, but I promised my girls we would do a sleepover tonight."

"All good. Your friends are hot I would rather hang out with them too." Eli has grown especially fond of Madison. He hasn't made a move or anything, but maybe he'll finally lose his virginity. I tease him about it sometimes, but I mean well.

We made it all the way home with useless conversation. When Eli pulls in front of my house and unlocks the door, he says, "You've been off lately. Is everything okay?"

I'm confused. Does Eli have enough self-awareness to pick up on my change in demeanor? Have I had a change in my demeanor?

"I-," I hesitate is what I do. "I'm fine, yeah. My situationship and I have officially ended things." I think.

"If you ever want to talk about it Belle, you can with me."

My heart fills with warmth as I am left dumbfounded by his compassion.

Eli continues, "You don't always have to be strong in front of everyone."

My armor has been fading. People are starting to see who I am.

That doesn't sit right with me. I feel exposed. I choose to cut him short. "I really appreciate that, Eli," and I genuinely do. "I'll see you Monday. Thanks for the ride."

He calls after me, "See you Monday."

Act II

CHAPTER FOURTEEN

My Mom and I have been fine since the disagreement about our family trip. When we argue, we never dwell on it too long. That is, of course, until it comes back up. She bought me a bunch of chips and stuff to bring to Elena's tonight. That was nice of her. I didn't tell her that, though. She never lets me go anywhere empty-handed. Even if it's a routine sleepover with the friends I've had since kindergarten.

I'm out the door and heading to Elena's with a quick goodbye to my entire family. We're not planning on drinking tonight. I'm sure we'll smoke at some point. This sleepover was actually Kelly's idea. It's been a while since we did a night just the girls, and she thought it was important for bonding. The idea isn't totally awful, so now here I am.

Kelly, Madison, Elena, and I have already housed six orders of buffalo wings. Those are our favorites. Since we wasted no time hitting my weed pen, we had no choice but to order wings. We're getting bored, realizing we have a whole night together, just the four of us, and no alcohol. It feels inappropriate to do what little girls do at sleepovers. We're grown now, but what do big girls do at sleepovers instead? Elena suggested we text the boys, but Kelly rebutted that quickly. So, instead, we do what all teenage girls do best and divulge into the intricacies of our lives.

Madison announces, "I think I'm going to get with the guy in my Spanish three class. Every time he talks, all I can think about is sticking my tongue in his throat."

Our innocent giggles flood the space.

Elena's goofy ass agrees, "You do love your Spanish men."

"Girl!" Kelly interrupts, "Who doesn't? We all wish we could look a little more like Marabelle so that the Spanish men would attract to us naturally."

"I don't know, Kel, Spanish boys love white girls." Madison squeezes her tits and winks, "At least in my experience."

I can't stop laughing at these idiots. It's moments like this that remind me how much I love these girls.

"Bro, I haven't had sex in so long," I redirect the conversation so we're not all laughing at Madison feeling herself up anymore.

"How long?" Elena says with mockery.

"Probably like two days because Belle is a sex freak."

"Yeah, seriously, you would die without it, Belle."

I clear my name, "It's been three weeks, everyone shut the fuck up."

Shut the fuck up.

"Belle, are you kidding me," Kelly interjects. "I haven't had sex in 3 months! The crazy part is I haven't gotten my period."

"Are you an idiot? You mean you haven't gotten your period since the last time you had sex 3 months ago?" Elena screams.

Kelly clarifies, "No, no. Like I got my period after I had sex, and then I haven't gotten it for the

last three months. I'm not pregnant, you freak."
She laughs, "My doctor switched my birth control. It's prob from that."

"Imagine she was pregnant?" I say.

Madison takes a huge inhale from my pen. Exhaling, she breathes, "Thank god she's fucking not."

We all laugh. My laugh gradually fades. I haven't gotten my period in a while. How long has it been? I'm on birth control. There's no way I could get pregnant.

"I haven't gotten my period either," I share.

Elena's eyes fill with panic.

I grab her arm. "Relax, there's literally no way."

"You're on the pill, right?" She presses me.

"Yes, of course."

Kelly and Madison turn to each other, plotting. Rejoining Elena and I, they say, "Let's go take a test."

Madison continues, "We'll all take one." She mocks in an oval voice, "To all make sure we're not pregnant."

Not much thought is given by any of us. We all agree to go. It's funny. It'll give us something to do.

"We can get more snacks while we're there, too," Elena obliges.

"Perfect, I'll drive." They all get into my car.

———— · ⚘ · ————

The drugstore we pull into is dead. I guess not many people need pregnancy tests or Skittles at eleven p.m. on a Friday. I think we're all relieved to see that it'll be the workers judging us and not any other shoppers. Four teenage girls walking into a drugstore to buy pregnancy tests isn't something you see too often. It's normally Saturday morning when the panic starts to settle, and you have to run out for a plan B. I've never taken a plan B before. I've never had to. Jace and I have had no problems in that department. I know Elena has a couple of times. She's a little more reckless than I am. She's explaining to me now that every time she's taken the morning-after pill, she gets pretty sick.

Kelly jumps in, "Well, yeah, it's basically like taking an entire pack of birth control at once. That shit's gotta be poison."

I interject, "I don't think they would give it to us if it were poison."

"If by they you mean the government, then oh yes, they would," Madison declares. "Let's grab our snacks first and then the tests."

I grab sour gushers, my favorite. I can't wait to hit my pen again and get lulled into the gushy explosion of goodness. Looking to my right and left, I realize everyone else must've made their way to the feminine care aisle. Rounding the corner, Elena has her phone pointed at them, cracking up.

"Come get yours, Belle," Elena switches the camera to me, "in case one of them is positive, we can start a family channel, and this will be the first video."

"People make a fortune off of those," Kelly ensures.

I reach for the test. It's lighter than I expected. It weighs nothing. How could something so powerful feel so pitiful?

I might still be high from before cause I'm not exactly sure what happens next. I think we all did self-checkout. I think we all laughed our asses off like this was one big bit. I think we're back at Elena's house and have all peed on our sticks.

The sound of Madison's chewing has consumed me. All I can hear is how she side-shuffles her jaw, gnawing on her milk duds. Who even eats milk duds anymore?

"We flip over on three," Elena says.

"one.."

There's no way I'm pregnant.

"two.."

Why the fuck did I agree to take this stupid test.

"three.."

"I'm good's" go off like fireworks around the room. Sparklers of laughter erupt for the finale of the show.

I can't move.

NO. NO. NO.

no.

I barely make out the three syllables, "It's positive."

Elena snatches it from my hand.

Madison launches herself forward to look over Elena's shoulder.

Kelly comes to me.

"It has to be a false positive.."

"Those can happen, right?"

"There's two lines though, Elena." Madison grabs it, "Look."

"Mine came with two; why don't you take it again, Belle? I'm sure it's a mistake." Kelly reaches into the cardboard for her second test.

"Oh good, those digital ones are more accurate," Madison says.

Good. I don't feel so good.

I go to the bathroom without saying a word. I pee on the stick. The purple daisies that paint the walls suffocate me. What an awful choice for wallpaper. I stare at the three dots blinking back at me.

loading…..

loading….

loading…

The box says to wait three minutes. My heart is inside my stomach, and my head can't begin to comprehend what the fuck is happening. I hear hushed whispers from the girls in the bedroom. I am becoming the host for their panic. I need to take from something because right now, I can feel nothing. They're concerned, scared even. They didn't expect this to happen. Neither did I.

loading...

The gray letters display on the screen. PREGNANT.

My body keeps me moving forward. I exit the bathroom, holding the test up like a pathetic participation award. That's all I was, a participant.

"Oh my god," Elena gasps.

"There's no way," Madison and Kelly repeat, "there's just no way. How is this even possible."

"This was supposed to be a joke. Something we were all going to laugh about. You guys shouldn't have suggested we take them." Elena is trying to find something to blame. Madison and Kelly are an easy target. After all, it was their idea.

I start laughing because if I don't laugh, I'll cry. This is a joke. It was supposed to be a joke. I was waiting to flip a negative test, laugh with all of them, and enjoy my sour gushers. I finally speak. "I'm on the pill, so I have no idea what's going on right now. Jace never even nuts in me. He always pulls out."

"I guess sometimes," Elena trails off, "mistakes happen. What should we do?"

"Um, I -I." I stumble. "I think I'm just going to go. This is all happening so fast. I should probably call Jace. I don't really know what I'm going to say."

Madison's sad for me. "Do you want to call him here, and we'll go to another room? You shouldn't be alone right now, Belle."

"I'm fine, really. I'm sorry I brought the mood down." Everyone's staying so quiet, proceeding with extreme caution.

Kelly pleads, "Belle, do not be sorry; this is no one's fault." Tears form in her eyes. " Those tests don't mean anything; you need a real doctor to check if you're pregnant or not."

I cannot be here when her tears fall. I cannot be here any longer. I want them to forget this whole thing ever happened. I say, "Just you know, don't say anything to anyone. This stays between us." I don't trust them. I grab the two positive tests. "And Elena, delete that video," I say firmly.

I buy two more boxes of tests on the way home. I pee on every stick. Every stick is positive. Okay, so six tests, six pregnants, I need to call Jace. I thought maybe they were wrong, both of them. I thought maybe I could have been hallucinating the last two hours, but with six in front of me, it's getting tough to deny.

I call Jace. No answer.

I call Jace again. No answer.

I stare at my phone, lost in the void of trying to puzzle together when this could've happened. I fucked Jace about three weeks ago when he randomly showed up at my house the night of Madison's party. I also fucked him a couple of weeks before that. Did I get my period in between those two fucks? I can't remember. But even when we fucked three weeks ago, he pulled out and came on my ass. Or was it my stomach? Did he come on my stomach the time before? Why the fuck can't I remember where the fuck he came?

He texts me:

Jace: I'm at a party right now. What do you want?

I call again. No answer.

I call again.

"What, Marabelle, what the fuck do you need that can't wait? I'm a little busy right now."

"I'm pregnant." If I have to know, so does he.

"Ha ha, very funny. Go waste someone else's time with your bullshit."

I take a picture of the tests in my lap and send it to him. "Look at your texts."

He pauses long enough for me to hear the loud music and bitches giggling in the background. "I don't believe you." Jace is angry. "It's not mine. You had to have fucked someone else. This is not my problem, Marabelle."

I'm crushed. "What do you mean it's not yours? I only fuck you, Jace. I wouldn't have fucking called you if this isn't our problem." The tears start to run down my cheeks. I thought I could call him to help make sense of whatever the fuck is happening inside of my body. That I had absolutely no knowledge of until two hours ago. I don't know what to do, what to say. I'm only eighteen. I can't be pregnant. Now he's going to flip this on me like this is my fucking fault. I need him right now, and he's making it damn hard to get near him.

"You're ruining my night Marabelle. I'll come up tomorrow, and we can talk about whatever you think is going on," Jace demands.

"What the fuck Jace. I literally just found out I'm pregnant. I'm fucking terrified out of my mind." My voice trembles, "I-I-I can't wait until tomorrow."

"You're going to have to because that's when I can see you." He hangs up.

Three beeps end the call. I throw the tests off myself. I use my arms as a swaddle around my body. I hold myself there, sobbing, until my soul leaves my body.

CHAPTER FIFTEEN

Three things have happened between last night and this morning. One, I ate pancakes with my Mom and sister. My sister requested pancakes, I benefited from that request, and my Mom made pancakes. We ate like normal. We talked like normal. My Mom was so excited about a new syrup she grabbed at the store today—some chatter about how it's organic and supposed to be better for you. I started to consider that everyone says pregnant women can't eat certain things. Can I not eat certain things now? I've been smoking and drinking more than usual, so I don't think the syrup will make a difference. Oh my god, I've been smoking and drinking this whole time. How have I not killed it? Is that how that works?

I cleaned up the kitchen in thanks to my Mom for making us breakfast. It was something to distract my mind. I can't think about anything else. My sister has a dance competition today. I would usually go but I told my Mom I have to run lines with Eli. Lie. I actually have to tell Jace I'm pregnant, this time in person.

Two, Jace texted me early this morning that he would be at my house around 2:30 pm. Despite his leisurely arrival time, the text was sent at 6:48 am. I wonder if he's been up all night, too.

Three, all I want to eat is a sesame bagel with hot sauce and cream cheese. I hate cream cheese. I always have. The creepy white color paired with the sour, rotten taste has never been my cup of tea. I hate spicy shit too. Anytime I've ever had it, my whole face gets red, and I wind up sneezing a hundred times. Yet here I am. My body could commit murder for that bagel. It's like since I took the test, my body and mind have made the connection that we're pregnant. All the symptoms have come flooding in after six positive tests. It could be a placebo. I could be making up the cravings. It's like Stockholm syndrome inside my own body—this thing in me, the captor, and I, the victim.

Please don't ask how long it's been because I don't know. I know I've watched five episodes of Love Island. I know I haven't gotten up to pee in a while. I know I've looked at my bong a thousand times and can't bring myself to hit it. I'm not having this thing anyway; it shouldn't matter. I know that it's 2:45 pm, and Jace still isn't here. I tried to cry a few times today but my eyes are broken. I will not cry when he gets here.

My phone dings:

Jace: I'm here

Is he not coming in? I'm confused.

Me: I'll be down in 5

I throw on whatever and grab all the tests as my alibi's. He's pulled over a couple of houses away from mine. Parked. Neither one of us says anything as I get into the car. He looks at the tests in my hands. I hand them to him.

He flips each one over, inspecting them like I'm a part of a case study. He hands them back to me and says, "You're sure it's mine?"

"Yes, I'm sure."

"Well, we haven't been together in a while, so it could be someone elses. Is it Nick's?"

It must've bothered him if he cared to remember his name.

"It's yours. I wouldn't do this to you if it wasn't."

Jace takes a long inhale. "There has to be a clinic open today," he starts typing on his phone, "I can take you now."

Clinic open, today? I found out less than 24 hours ago. I'm pretty sure I want to have an abortion, but I'm not positive. I don't know what I know, but I think a decision like this needs more than 24 hours to process.

"I know a friend who went through this. I called him this morning," he's talking fast. "He said this place is open 24 hours, 7 days a week. I'm going to call and see if they could take you to have the abortion today."

Did he just make my decision for me? I nod along because I'm not in complete control of my spirit anyway. He's giving me more than he was last night. I'll take what I can get. The phone blares through his old car speakers. The beat of my heart feels louder than every stereo combined. We both wait.

"Hello, this is Micah from Planned Parenthood. How can I assist you?" The woman's voice is chirpy.

"Hi, um, do you guys accept walk-ins?" Jace asks.

"Yes, we do, sir."

"Would we be able to come in today?" Another question.

"We have a high volume of patients booked for today, so we are not accepting any walk-ins. I apologize, but I suggest scheduling your appointment now or first thing Monday morning." She's typing. Getting ready to insert my name into a document. "Will your partner be getting a DNC or treatment with the pills?"

I shake my head at him and mouth to hang up.

Jace continues on the phone, "Thank you, but we're going to call back Monday morning."

"Okay, stay well!" And the line cuts out.

"So what do you want to do?" He turns to me, "I can look up another place."

"I want to pause for a second. Do you even know how much this is going to cost? There is no way I can go through insurance. My Mom will see the charge come through on the bill. I have money from my summer job that I can take out of my account, but I can't take out a lot without it being suspicious. My Mom is linked to my account, Jace."

He interrupts, "It's going to be expensive if you don't go through insurance. Why don't you figure out how to get the money, and I'll find a place to go to." I'm feeling a little better knowing he believes me now.

I start to cry. He doesn't react. This is all too overwhelming.

"What made you take a test?" He asks genuinely.

"All the girls and I were joking around. They thought it would be funny if we all took one."

"How is this even possible?" He says defeated.

"I don't know, Jace. I've been trying to figure that out." I scream, "I'm on the pill for fucks sake. And you never nut in me."

Jace looks apologetic. The wheels begin to turn in his mind. "I-" he hesitates, "I think I might have nut in you a little the last time."

"WHAT! You didn't think to tell me?"

"It wasn't a big deal. I pulled out a little late and nut on your stomach. I saw a little bit drip out of you but I didn't know if it was yours or mine. And I figured if it was coming out, it wasn't staying in."

"What the fuck is wrong with you? How could you not even mention it? It's my body, Jace, and I trusted you with it. I would like to know what goes on, even if I can't see it," I'm pissed. "Especially if I can't see it."

His smooth, know-it-all-all attitude is begging for help right now. "I don't fucking know anything. I knew you were on the pill. I didn't know a drop of cum could get someone pregnant. Did you?" He's screaming right back at me. "How do I know you were taking your birth control at the right time every day? You're always forgetting to bring it with you when you go places. There's no point in pointing fingers right now, Marabelle. You're fucking pregnant, and I'm only nineteen," he wavers. "We can't have a fucking baby."

"Obviously, I'm not going to keep it," I suck in a breath, "but you could've at least given me the option."

He doesn't even realize he's done it. Instilled his power over me the minute this whole thing broke loose.

"I'm just as scared as you are right now. The right and wrong thing is getting very blurry for me."

"I know," I whisper. A bomb has hit the both of us. There is no use in us fighting this battle separately. There's strength in numbers, right? And now it's me, and it's him, and it's this thing inside me.

He hasn't touched me since I got into the car. It's odd that we're even in his car to begin with. He's only made eye contact with me once. That was when the lady wanted to schedule me in. It's like we're both here, but I can no longer feel his presence.

I turn my whole body towards him, "Why didn't you want to come in?"

"Because this doesn't mean we're together now. We weren't together when I fucked you, and we're not together now. Yes, you're pregnant, and I'll fix that, but this doesn't change shit between us."

Jace's conversational whiplash has left me wounded.

"Do you even understand what is happening right now? I have a baby starting to form inside of me. A baby that you and I have made together."

"Yeah, I fucking got that Belle. If you can't get it done today, then there's no point in you still being in my car." He unlocks the doors, "Figure out the money, for now. I'll pay you back when I have it and let you know. Then we can find a place."

He doesn't want to come in? Doesn't want to hug me? Doesn't want to tell me everything is going to be okay? He doesn't want me?

Jace

"FUCKK!!" I scream over and over again. Banging my fists into my steering wheel until my knuckles take the brunt of my pain. I see red, and I feel black. What the fuck have I done. How could I have been so stupid, so selfish? I claimed her body like it was my own like it belonged to me, and she obliged every goddamn time. She's pregnant, and I'm fucked. She can't have it; I have to make sure that she doesn't have it. We can't be parents, and we can barely get along long enough to have a legitimate conversation. It's fun and playful, and one of the things I love most about her, but that's no environment for a child.

I was planning on driving straight back to school, but I don't know if I can right now. This is embarrassing, shameful. I've been fucking Belle for years, we never ever had a scare. Now, I'm in full panic mode. All she did today was cry. She looked horrible. She sounded even worse. I couldn't look at her. I was so disgusted with myself for doing this to her. I also didn't know if I could look at her without my eyes going directly to her stomach like there would already be something to see. When she called me last night, I was caught up in my own shit. A fight had broken out between my roommate Oliver and the frat boy whose house it was. I had to step in, of course, to break it up before we got thrown out of the party. I got pushed around a little bit, but nothing I'm not used to. Belle called me right after that. I left the party immediately and threw up everything I had on the sidewalk. It could've been from all the liquor I ingested but news like that won't leave anyone stable.

I called one of my old buddies from high school when I made it back to the dorms. I remember him going through the same thing with his girl a little over a year ago. He's not somebody I talk to daily, but I knew he would have my back. I gave him the facts, everything I knew. Nothing of how I felt. He told me about that clinic I called early. Clearly, they're very busy with a plethora of abortions to administer. So now I suffer. After I called him last night, I broke down. I don't usually react to things this compromised. This one though, I couldn't control. It kept bubbling and bubbling waiting to be heard. I would love a family with Belle. I would adore her for the rest of my life, but not now. I need more freedom until I'm ready to settle down. I know that she'll be the one I end up with. I also know that doesn't have to be today. That's one of the reasons I never officially asked her to be my girlfriend. It crushes her. She'll be my endgame. I'm just not ready to end the game.

I want to tell my Mom about this whole thing, she would know what to do. If my shame wasn't louder than my pride then I would. Nobody can know. Marabelle better keep her prissy little friends in order because I won't have this news all over the town. I'm a respectable guy; my reputation would be ruined.

A final look around this god-forsaken town, and I decide I need to get out of here. I keep getting sucked back here like I'm a premium member of the vortex. I wonder if every town has its own vortex with people and things that will always circle back to you and drag you down. I will not let this pregnancy drag me down. I'll give Belle the money for the abortion once I have it. I can't be here. I need to get back to school. I have a lot of work to do and more important responsibilities. Midterms will be here before I know it. I can't afford to get behind on work. I'll bring her the money when I have it. She can take care of it. She's strong. She'll book the appointment, go in, get it out, and this whole thing will be over.

CHAPTER SIXTEEN

I go to school. I go to all my classes. I even go to rehearsal. I sing. I dance. I talk and laugh like I normally would. I had to go to school today. My world would have never resumed if I hadn't gone to school today. I have to keep moving. I have to keep my life as is because nothing is different. Once this is all over, everything will go back to the way it was. I will start to feel normal again.

When Jace left yesterday, I didn't know I could feel worse about the situation. I sat on my bathroom floor, refusing to look at myself in the mirror. I can't even bring my eyes to look at what may or may not be there.

Elena called me a couple of times. I answered once. The other girls haven't said a word to me.

I'm hoping Elena has told them that what she heard from me isn't good and they should back off. I'm going to Elena's after school today. She said she was going to help me figure everything out.

I got out of rehearsal fifteen minutes ago. I must be moving in slow motion because I'm pulling up to Elena's a little late. She opens the door before I even get close to the front.

"Hey, you okay? I thought you get out of practice at 5?" Elena says.

"Yeah, I'm fine. I got caught up with Eli." I lie.

We make our way into her bedroom, but this feels off. She's like waiting for me to explode or something. I feel fragile around her, weak. I've never felt either one of those things around my best friend. I am the strong one. This is all fucked up.

I break the ice. "So you really think you can spot me the money. It will only be for a little bit. I don't want anything to look suspicious coming out of my account."

"I can spot you until you have it. You know my Mom doesn't give a fuck about money, so she won't bat an eye. Besides, if she does, I'll say I did some extra spring shopping." She rubs my arm, "It'll be no big deal."

"Thank you 'cause Jace said he would get me the money, but I don't know when that will be. So you'll pay for it, and then once I get the money from him, I'll give it to you. It's going to be like $500. I've been doing a lot of googling."

Since my extensive Google search, I've concluded that I have no idea what I'm getting myself into. I didn't know there are two different kinds of abortions, and I definitely don't know which one is better. Why are there two? One says that you have to go under general anesthesia, but the other one just says something about taking a couple of pills. I don't fucking know. There's not much information on either one, to be honest. They're all written in doctor jargon that I do not understand. I would like a step-by-step of what is going to happen to me. None of them tell me what's the best procedure for an eighteen-year-old girl who is lost and terrified and wants this thing gone.

I turn to Elena, fear smeared on my face. "Do you think, maybe, we could tell your Mom? I can't tell my Mom cause that's like every Mom's worst nightmare, and I'm already really close to your Mom. I feel like she would know what to do. Or at least help me with which one to get. She's so chill. I think I can trust her with this. I really would much rather die than have to inform anyone else about this, but it's a huge decision and I don't want to make the wrong one." A tear drops. "I need an adult to tell me what to do."

"Let's tell my Mom, Belle; she'll know what to do." Elena hugs me. I let her. "Do you—would you want to keep it?"

No one has asked me that.

"No, I don't want to keep it," I say hesitantly. "I-I-It's starting to feel real, like I'm actually pregnant. I can't keep it. I can't have a baby, Elena. And with Jace?? We cannot have a baby. What kind of life would that be for a child?"

She shakes her head in reassurance, "No, I know. I had to ask."

"I don't know if I'm making the right decision, but the faster this gets done, the better off I will be."

An hour goes by before we head downstairs to talk with Elena's Mom. Elena has done most of the talking. I think I've said a couple of words. I'm kind of unsure at this point. My heart was beating so fast that it was hard to hear the words coming out of Mrs. Gonzalez's mouth. She insisted we print out what I've found about both kinds of abortions. She thought it would be helpful to see them on paper. So that's what we're doing now, looking through abortions like it's a magazine.

Mrs. Gonzalez pushes the papers towards me. "Have you ever been under anesthesia, honey?"

"No, that's what I would be afraid of. If I did that one."

"General anesthesia is very simple. It feels like a deep sleep. I understand your hesitancy especially if you don't want your Mom to have any part of this. God for bid something goes wrong they, would need to call her."

"Yeah, exactly. I can't have that."

"Okay," she continues. "So it's looking like the pills are your best bet. This place here," she points to her computer, "has good reviews."

"Okay, yeah, I-um-I'll call and make the appointment now."

"You want to do it right now, sweetie?" She asks.

"Yeah, they're going to close soon, and I don't want to wait a whole nother day."

Mrs. Gonzalez shuts the computer slowly, "Marabelle, have you considered keeping this baby?"

Baby.

"I know this is a lot right now," she pries. "But you don't seem a hundred percent sure. This is a huge decision, and I would hope that you're a hundred percent. You could always go through the adoption process if you don't think keeping it is in your best interest. I'm positive that Jace would step up if he knew you are deciding to keep it."

I'm at gunpoint. This is an ambush. Every single part of my body is screaming to run. I look at Elena. She apologizes with her eyes. She didn't know her mother would have this opinion.

Everyone is going to have an opinion about how I handle this. The world is so up in arms about it for a reason.

I audibly exhale and grab options A and B from the table. The papers and my car keys crammed into my hand. I stand. "I appreciate your help, Mrs. Gonzalez. I think I'm going to get going."

"I didn't mean to offend you, sweetie. A baby could be a blessing. You might not be able to see that right now."

A fucking blessing. She must be incapable of sympathy because I feel anything but fucking blessed. I've been paying respects to my casket on repeat since I flipped over that godforsaken stick.

"I don't want to have a baby Mrs. Gonzalez. I hope you can respect my decision."

Elena faces me, "I'll call you later, Belle."

"Yeah," I say and walk out of their home.

CHAPTER SEVENTEEN

This tight, compressed sports bra digs into me like a punishment. *It has to be a placebo effect.*

I came to open gym tonight because I need to be anywhere else except home. I called the abortion clinic with "good reviews." I have an appointment for Thursday at 9 am. Elena is going to take me because they drilled into my skull that they cannot release me unless someone is there to accompany me. My companion told me he didn't want to come with me. He thinks it's best if I go with Elena. Expect Elena didn't get me pregnant. Elena and I aren't in love, or so I thought we were. I'm not really sure what happened to us figuring this out together.

It's like it's not happening to him. He seemed so accommodating the other day. Like he was eager to tackle this problem together.

Whatever. I need to keep punching things. I have on the same little sports bra and leggings from the first time Nick took me here. That day with Nick feels awfully long ago.

The instructors here change every time. I'm still a beginner, so they've got me learning basic positioning and blocks. As soon as I step into the gym, I'm calm. This place takes me out of my head and puts me in the present. I want to follow directions. I want to be good at this.

Different groups occupy every mat. I scan the gym once to check if Nick is there. He's not.

My braids are soaking with sweat. I worked hard enough today that I'm ready to get out of here. The open gym is very casual; you can come and go as you please. That's one of the things I love about this place. It's so laid back.

At the end of class, my trainer told me my punch was getting more power. He's proud of me. If only he knew the change behind the power. I was punching like the Hulk tonight with the amount of aggression I have festering inside of me.

I pull the tape from my hands. Circling them with each other to release the sticky fiber from my skin. My eyes do another scan over the space. Nick is starting to wipe down the mats in the far left corner. When did he get here? Does he know I'm here? Nick doesn't work here or anything, but from what I've gathered, this is his family. He spends most of his time at this gym.

My anxious thoughts try to crack the calm state I entered during practice. I push it down. At this point, Nick feels like a ghost to me. He was mad at me at Madison's party, but I didn't know it would last this long. To be fair, I have had a lot going on and haven't reached out, but still, I thought he was into me.

I toss on my flannel and zip my bag. I get so close to backing out. This is his safe space that he invited me into. I don't want him to feel like I'm intruding by being here. I'm overthinking this. Nick is different than Jace. He wants me to say hi. I can't be a coward and walk away.

"Hey, Nick," I say, approaching him.

"Marabelle, hi." He tosses the dirty wipes into the garbage. "How was your class?"

"It was really good. I feel like I'm finally starting to get the hang of it."

"I'm sure you are. You've been coming for the last couple of weeks. The more consistent you stay with it, the better you'll get."

I smirk. "How'd you know I've been coming the last few weeks?"

"I have my sources," he says with a laugh. "I had to know if I got you even a little interested."

"Well, you did." My hands flare out to the space around me. "I really do love it here. It's been my saving grace lately."

Why do I want to tell him? Why do I want to collapse in his arms and tell him the biggest secret I'll ever keep? This boy barely knows me, and yet I can see our endless lifetimes through his eyes.

"Do you want to grab some food? I haven't eaten dinner yet and wouldn't mind the company."

"I would love some food right now. But Nick," I pause. "You have to let me pay."

"And why's that?" He teases.

"It's my apology for Madison's party. For standing you up."

"Fine." He lets out with a sigh. "Let's go."

He suggested we get take out and eat at his place. I obliged because, lately, the fewer decisions I have to make, the better. I like that I don't think much around Nick. He goes, and I follow. He's dominant without being controlling. He's not Jace.

"I can't believe you ate that whole freakin thing. I'm impressed, girl," he chuckles.

"I was hungry, and I hadn't eaten all day." I push his arm playfully. "It was a huge burrito though."

We both laugh, knowing that not many girls would've taken down that whole burrito, especially in front of a guy. I feel so at peace. In my sweaty gym clothes, frizzy braids, and a full belly, *literally*. This is the most I've laughed in a while.

He offers me his joint. I hesitate. I'm known as the girl who smokes a lot of weed. Recently, I've been declining. I didn't know how smoking would affect the baby. I guess it doesn't matter since I'm getting an abortion on Thursday. I take the joint from him.

Through the joint exchange, we have made our way closer to each other on his sofa. It seems like Nick lives in the basement. We came in through the basement door. There's only a sofa and bed down here. The bedroom door is ajar. I can see his half-made bed through the crack. I guess we didn't eat in there strategically.

My problems fade away with the cloud of smoke that wisps its way through the cracked window above our heads. His hand rests on my thigh once he's put the joint out. I lay my leg over his.

"So, do you forgive me now?" I ask.

"For what?"

"For Madison's Nick."

He draws imbecilic circles on my thigh. "I never resented you for it. I was disappointed, yes, but never mad at you." He explains.

"I was starting to think you were a figment of my imagination. I haven't seen you anywhere."

"Maybe you were looking in all the wrong spots," his finger traces higher and higher.

Taunting me. "I'm glad you didn't walk out of that gym tonight without saying anything."

My fucking body is on fire. I'm trying to move his finger with my mind.

Higher. Higher. Higher.

"I almost did," I place my hand on his cheek. "But you make me feel fearless."

He kisses me. Unforgiving. I join him with the same passion we have been longing for. It's a kiss that wakes up a deep urge inside me. I can feel him so beautifully real as he lapses his tongue over mine. His hand moves higher, cooperating with the manipulation of my mind. He teases me, mocking those same circles he was provoking on my thigh.

A moan escapes my throat that he poetically catches in our kiss. "Does that feel good?" He whispers into my ear. "You like when I tease you?"

"Yes," I gasp breathlessly. "Keep doing that."

His fingers keep moving as he drags his tongue along the side of my neck. Stopping at my ear, he says, "Can I take these off of you?" Tugging gently on the band of my leggings.

I nod and let him drag my leggings off of my hips. I never thought consent could be so hot.

He observes me bare in my thong before coming back to me. "God, you're so fucking beautiful, Marabelle."

Where the fuck did this man come from? I've never felt so wanted in my life.

Nick gently moves my underwear to the side. The cold air against my hot flesh turns me on even more. His fingers explore until they find their way back to my center. He's insufferably gentle in the way he touches me. We kiss, he teases me, we kiss again. I want to feel him.

I reach my hand over his sweatpants to feel the entire length of him. He's already hard, already ready for me. I start to tease him to see how he likes to be touched. The expression of his pleasure grows. We're lost in the art of each other, pausing to gaze at one another. We're not doing much to each other, but it's the way we've both wholly surrendered.

I push his pants away and wrap my hand over his flesh. It's so hard I can feel his dick pulsing in my palm. I continue to jerk him off as he says to me, "Belle, you're going to make me cum if you keep doing that."

I don't stop. I increase my speed. I need to feel this power. "Then come for me," I declare, kissing him down his neck.

He comes all over my leg.

As soon as he's finished, we both start giggling.

"This is embarrassing. I just came from you jerking me off like I'm in eighth grade and have never had my dick touched." He stands, grabbing a towel and wiping me clean.

"It's not embarrassing," I stand, meeting him, "I'm flattered, really," a chuckle escapes my lips.

He grabs my face, laughing, "You really turn me on."

"Me too."

"It's your turn," he says, brushing his thumb along my cheek.

Oh no. What have I done? *I'm pregnant.* I just hooked up with Nick. Nick, who's not Jace. I hate feeling this weight of what I did under the circumstances I've been given.

I want to, I really fucking want to, but not tonight.

"I'm actually okay. That was like really hot, but I'm okay with not coming."

He's caught off guard but doesn't press.

I continue, "Can we just like—" I take a moment. "You want to cuddle for a little before I go?"

"I would love that," he says, picking me up and returning to the sofa.

He does say another word. Taking a long sigh, I sink into his chest and rub my hands up and down each crater of muscle marking his torso. I want to be buried here in Nicholas Ricci's arms.

CHAPTER EIGHTEEN

Five more minutes until I can go home. The last five minutes of every class are always the slowest minutes of your life. I've glanced up at this clock 700 times, and I swear it has only ticked one mark over. That's not possible. Tick. Tick Tick. Every clock in a school has to be specially crafted, crafted for terror. There is no way that these clocks work like every other clock does.

You want these kinds of clocks when you're on your deathbed. To get those last precious moments here on earth. To tell your loved ones you love them. To watch the clock tick slowly before death comes to get you. I like to believe dying is a really peaceful moment. I feel like I'm dying. In this classroom. Staring at this clock.

The blaring bell sounds off in the speakers, and students move without thinking. I round the corner to find Elena already waiting for me at my locker. Nothing needs to be said as we approach the main office. We each sign ourselves out, ignoring the passive-aggressive comments from our very nasty secretary. We're eighteen, and the rule is that once you're eighteen, you can sign yourself out for any reason at any point during the day without parental consent. So I don't know why it's always so shocking to Ms. Attitude.

I didn't want to miss the first two periods this morning. It wouldn't have hurt my grades or anything. I just thought if I had to watch the clock tick all morning, I would rather do it with the distraction of my peers. Elena said it was completely up to me. She's been saying that since the day I sat down with her mom. I get what she's trying to do.

I get comfortable in the passenger seat. She has the money, I have my body, we're ready to get an abortion.

My mind has been everywhere the last couple of days. I can't believe I hooked up with Nick while I'm pregnant. I sort of feel guilty about it, like I did something wrong. Once I found out I was pregnant, my mindset around my body seemed to change instantly. There's a deep sense of protection and obligation that has crept its way into my conscious brain.

Nick texted me last night and asked if I wanted to hang out after school today. I told him I had a doctor's appointment and couldn't. Obviously, he felt what I did that night, or he wouldn't be so adamant about hanging out again.

My phone buzzes in my hand.

Nick: I hope everything's okay. Good luck at the doctor. I'll see you next week for open gym.

Fucking please don't do this to me. *He's so- nice, kind, sweet, amazing.* He's got to be a damn physic. I don't even break a smile. I know I don't deserve to.

Me: Thanks Nick, means a lot <3.

I assume Nick wouldn't be very comfortable with the idea of hooking up with me while I'm pregnant with some other guy's kid. I'm not comfortable with it. I'm never going to tell him that I was pregnant, or that I was pregnant the first time we hooked up.

Regardless of the whole guilty pregnancy thing, it was a perfect night. God, did he make me feel good. There was a sense of security and safety. I was totally there with him, nothing else on my mind. Jace only crept into my thoughts when they all came tumbling through. I haven't told anyone about it. It'll just be more ammunition to form opinions about me.

"Have you heard from Jace?" Elena snaps me out of my head.

"Eh," I shrug, "Let me read you our texts. It will be easier than explaining."

I swipe out of the conversation with my sweet Nicholas and bring up Jace's. "So two days ago, I texted him that I was getting it done today, and he said again that he didn't want to go. Then blah blah blah, he brings it back to how it's not his."

Elena rolls her eyes.

"I said I'm not fighting with you whether it's yours or not. I don't want this just as much as you don't. So, do you want to be a part of this or not?"

"Exactly!" Elena exclaims, "He's so fucking back and forth, like is he supporting you or not?"

"Yeah. So he says: Obviously, I don't want to be, but if you say it's mine, I guess I'm a part of it. I responded, okay, thanks for the support."

Elena inhales rage.

"Wait, no, it gets better." I continue, "He says, Okay. Just let me know when it's done and how much I gotta pay."

"What the fuck is wrong with him? He is giving you absolutely no support. He's saying it like he's forced to be a part of it. But what is he even doing for you? He only texts you when you text him first, and the way he's like, let me know when it's done?" She exhales. "That's so rude. He's an asshole."

My reaction is much more muted than how I feel. "He's treated me poorly the last couple of years, but never did I ever think he would treat me like this. I'm pregnant, we're pregnant, and he hasn't asked me once if I'm okay."

He was ready to tackle the problem so urgently. Once it couldn't disappear immediately, he cowardly retreated.

"I'm so sorry this is happening to you, Belle. It will all be over today, I promise."

There are moments in life when you are given a choice. The choice to have an abortion is often talked about in our society. It should be the woman's choice whether she wants to keep the child or not. It is up to the woman to decide what she wants to do with her own body. I believed all of those things until it was my body. I don't have a choice whether I go through with this or not. It was never a question of which choice I was going to make until the choice was taken away from me. It wasn't until Jace assumed I had made my choice that I realized I even had one.

All of these women are here for the same reason. This building has only one function. We're seated next to each other with our trusted companions to get us there and home and yet not many of us are surrounded by men. There is one man in a sea full of women. They appear to be an older couple. I noticed the diamond beaming on her finger and the band around his. Presence fills their eyes like this is the most painful thing they are about to do. The rest of us look like our consciousness has washed up on a deserted island. Our bodies will be back later to come pick us up. We'll have to hang on until then.

"Marabelle." The lady in blue scrubs announces from the entryway. I already told Elena I don't want her to come in with me. I'm fine to do it alone. I rise like this is the damn reaping, and whatever happens through those doors will leave a permanent mark on me.

"How are you doing today?" Blue Scrubs asks.

"Good." I actually might puke because of how anxious I am. I'm doing horrible Blue Scrubs, HORRIBLE.

"You can have a seat right here," she motions to the chair opposite her desk. "We have to run through some standard questions before starting."

We go through the generic name, date of birth, payment plan, etc.

She continues, "How far along do you think you are?"

"I'm not sure."

"Was it consensual?"

"Yes."

"At any point during intercourse, did you want to stop?"

"No."

"Did you use a condom?"

"No."

"Was this your first sexual encounter?"

"No."

"Is your partner with you today?"

"No."

"Is he aware you are getting this procedure done?"

"Yes."

"Are you sure you want to proceed with the abortion?"

I hesitate, "Yea."

"Okay, Marabelle, we'll just have to prick your finger and grab a blood sample before going into the other room."

A small pinch brings me slight contact with my physical body. It wasn't enough to keep me fully present.

It's cold in here. My nostrils burn from the smell of ethanol.

Blue Scrubs hands me a gown. "You can undress and put this on. The doctor will be in shortly."

I never see Blue Scrubs again.

How many women does she see a day? Asking those questions and pretending to offer an ounce of support, like she's on our side or something. Why do they ask all those questions anyway? She wrote down every single one of my answers. Now, my very complicated pain exists in a file somewhere.

Tick. Tick. Tick.

The clock blares inside my head. There's a subtle buzz that echos some warmth through these four walls.

I inhale. It has to have been fifteen minutes since Blue Scrubs told me to strip it down. How long do they keep you waiting in here, waiting for you to crack?

There's a knock at the door. I freeze. The itchy parchment cracking under me.

Peering around the door, Dark Blue Scrubs enters. That must be how they rank their superiority around here. Light Blue Scrubs means you ask the girls if they've been raped, and Dark Blue Scrubs means you remove the child.

What a fucked up job.

"Marabelle, good afternoon. I'm doctor—"

I don't know what her name is. I didn't care to hear her finish. I don't tune back in until she's shoving a twelve-inch wand up my vagina.

"We're going to do a quick examination to see how far along you are, and then we will proceed. This isn't going to hurt," she says as the cold is pressed inside me.

No words are spoken between us. She's looking at a monitor and probing that thing around inside. She clicks a few buttons on her screen.

Feeling the sun on your face is one of the most precious things we experience as humans. I could bask in the sun for hours. Feel the warm glow consume my being. As I lay here under this fluorescent lighting I feel the similarity of consumption. My eyes are locked on the buzzing lights above me. I will not look down. I will not look at that screen. Whatever she is seeing on that screen is going on inside my belly.

Removing the large stick, she announces, "Okay, Marabelle, why don't you go ahead and sit up for me." She snaps her gloves off. "So, unfortunately, we won't be able to do the procedure today. It appears you're only around five weeks pregnant. We recommend the pill being most effective at 8 weeks."

what?

"Can I get the other one then? The-the DNC?" I ask.

"We recommend the same time frame for both options." Dark Blue Scrubs, says.

Why can't I get it done today? Right now. Why the fuck does it matter if they're going to kill it anyway. Who the fuck came up with these rules? I came here. I stayed up all night anticipating this horrible day. I went to school to distract myself. I made a big fucking deal to Jace. I told him he would be off the hook after today. God, he's going to be so mad at me. I thought I did enough research. Everything said that an abortion can be done up to twelve weeks, especially the one with the pill. The internet never said anything about not being able to get it done too early. This is all too much. I'm confused. I'm overwhelmed. I feel fucking bamboozled.

"Excuse me, sweetheart, do you have any money you could spare?" A homeless man gets way too close to Elena.

We both get in the car as fast as possible, locking the doors and pulling away. He wouldn't back away from the car until we were on the street.

Elena gasps, "This is a really bad area."

Yeah. It is a bad area. It's a low-income area. The ghetto, some people call it. It's a place to keep minorities in their place. Of course, there is a planned parenthood in the middle of a low-income community. I guess I'm another stereotype. A Latina girl who got knocked up by a white boy, getting an abortion to slap another statistic on my face.

Except today, I didn't get one. Not much of what happened after Dark Blue Scrubs was memorable. I dressed. Floated back to the lobby and left. I told Elena I couldn't have it done today that I was only 5 weeks. She was trying to make sense of it but didn't believe them. That's when the homeless man tried to haggle us for money.

We've been talking about everything except what happened.

I couldn't book my next appointment on the way out. It's an embarrassment. Are all those people in the lobby who would listen to me ask to reschedule my abortion? They're going to wonder if I backed out. Should I back out? I'm going to go to a different place. I'll call and see if they can take me sooner.

The rest of the day is a blur of colors and sounds muddling together to create my reality. I ate dinner with my family. I spoke like I normally would. I focused on the play as much as possible. My sister likes hearing about it, and my parents just like that we carry the conversation for them. I have grown eternally grateful for what my mind has done for me. I can't be here, not in this physical plane. It's too much right now. My body has to forgive me one day.

Jace didn't text me or ask me how it went. Didn't ask if I was in pain or if I needed anything.

It's 3:47 a.m. I text him.

Me: Just wanted to let you know I couldn't get it done today. I'm only five weeks, I have to reschedule when I'm further along.

My eyes finally drift shut, allowing my exhaustion in.

It feels like an echo in my soul, but my phone dings me awake.

8:30 a.m. He responds.

Jace: Stop making it sound like you're actually pregnant all this talk about how far along you are just makes it seem like something's coming from it. That's fine. Let me know when it's done. I'll get the money to you before then.

I am actually pregnant. YOU actually got me pregnant. Five weeks indicates the amount of time I have lived with something growing inside me without my knowledge. Three weeks actually indicates how much longer I have to wait until I can get rid of this thing. And you, Jace, are making this harder than it already is.

I weep into my pillow. Attempting to drown out my screams, I don't want to go to school today. So I don't. I go back to sleep.

I shut it off.

6:42 p.m. I finally respond:

Me: Why are you acting like this? It's not about the money, Jace. I feel lost right now. This is hard enough.

He doesn't respond.

CHAPTER NINETEEN
Jace

I've drank every night this week. College is an adult playground, and I've been playing a lot. This is the third consecutive night I'm at the same frat house. These guys throw parties like it's their job. Even if it's not a big party, there are always people drinking here, no matter what day of the week. Girls trail these halls searching for their souls, and boys trail behind them, giving them anything but that.

Oliver comes with me some nights, but most nights when he knows I'm going out, he has a girl over. Oliver sleeps with a lot of women. I respect him for it, honestly. He plays a good game, I've definitely taken some notes from him. Tonight's typical roommate is out, time to bang situation for him. I'm sure he plans on doing exactly that.

I've been here for like two, maybe three hours. This one girl across the room has been eye fucking me all night. I've been doing it right back. Recently, my game has kind of been off. You know, my mind has been a little clustered. I think this little blonde will do the trick.

I can't think about it anymore; I can't feel the pressure of her needing me. What the fuck am I suppose to say to her? I couldn't believe she didn't get it done the other day, and when she texted me about it, she made it seem like only five weeks was way too early. The first thing I did after reading that text was Google when you can hear a baby's heartbeat. Five weeks. You can start to hear the heartbeat at five weeks. Did she hear the heartbeat? I can't know. I can't know. I can't know. Stop it. Stop it. Stop it. Stop thinking about it. Stop fantasizing about what a future would look like. She's not having it, and I don't fucking want her to. I have to keep telling myself it'll be over soon.

"I'm gonna roll up if anyone wants to smoke," I announce abruptly. I jolt off the couch, b-lining for the bathroom. I need to smoke. I need something.

The hot piss streams out of me, offering slight serenity. Going to the patio outside, I get my stuff set up on the table. I need something while I roll, or I'm going to fucking blow. There's a communal pack of cigarettes perfectly placed in the center of the table. Everything in this damn house is communal. The cigarette flame illuminates my face, and I inhale sharply. I don't smoke cigarettes often. I actually think they're kind of gross, but god, I love the way it makes me feel.

"Can I get a puff of that," Blondie appears out of nowhere.

I tip my head, granting her permission. We exchange the passing of the cigarette.

"I've seen you here the last couple of nights. You pledging the frat or something?" She asks.

"Fuck no," I laugh, "Frat guys are losers. I like to party, and they happen to host a lot of them."

"Hmm." She blows the smoke out, pursing her lips, begging to be fucked.

"What's your deal then? Why are you always here?" I question.

"I don't like to be alone." She says so candidly.

I grab my cig back from her, "At least you're honest." I shrug.

I don't care for this cigarette anymore. I'm much more interested in knowing why she followed me out here.

I start rolling, and she takes a seat on the table next to me. Her legs hang over the edge inches from my arm.

"I'm Grace," she chirps as I look up at her. "Since you were kind enough to ask me my name."

I lick the edges of the blunt, "I'm not kind, Grace. Never expect that from me."

Marabelle is always expecting things from me. She sets an exception that I never consented to. This is who I am. I am not kind.

I look her into Grace's eyes, "You've been eye fucking me all night. It's quite flattering," I add sarcastically.

She takes a beat, intrigued by my honesty. She looks at me with those sweet, demonic eyes. "Maybe I want to fuck you, Jace," Grace says flatly. "It is Jace, right?"

"Yeah, it's Jace. You mean to tell me, sweet little Grace has been observing me all night, thinking about all the ways you want to fuck me?" I toss the finished blunt on the tray in front of me. "It's been hours. You must have a very vivid imagination. So tell me this then, how many guys have you fucked in that room, Grace?" I stand in front of her, her legs naturally parting for me.

"Not one," she smirks leaning back on her hands. "I don't play games, Jace, but I can tell you do, so tell me, how hard am I going to have to work to get you to want me?"

Well, that's just the thing, Grace. I don't let myself want anyone. The second I want someone, I need them, and when I need them, it'll hurt too much when they decide to leave me. Marabelle has left me before. About a year ago, she had it with me. I thought the playful "we're together but not officially together" would always sort of be our thing. That was until she started asking questions about what I do when I go out with my friends. My lifestyle is the way I like it. I like to go out and party and maybe even flirt with a couple of girls. I might've taken it too far a couple of nights, and Belle was starting to feel it, I guess. But she left, blocked me, told me to go fuck myself. We didn't talk for like four months after that. That was the hardest shit I had to go through. I felt like I had been robbed of one of my senses. Walking around blind, wondering where the fuck my vision went? We came back to each other, but I never trusted her the same after that.

She has the strength to truly leave me. I don't.

I tower over this girl. She's pretty short, but she looks older in a mature way. She's gotta be at least a junior in college. I tend to attract a lot of older women. I'm not sure why.

I place my hand on Grace's waist. "Lucky for you, I'm in no mood tonight." Her breath hitches. I can feel her tense under my touch. I lean in to kiss her, and she wastes no time lacing her hands around my neck and pulling me in.

We find our rhythm shortly. She uses a lot of tongue in an attempt to please me. It's half working. My hands explore her body, noting her full chest and not-so-full ass.

You can't force passion. It's intangible.

Grace is trying to force it. I can taste the desperation on her tongue the longer we kiss. I can feel how badly she wants me to be the one. I can use her. Good lord, could I use some good head right now. I know Grace would give me that. She would shoot herself in the head if I told her to.

I squeeze her ass harder, trying to get a reaction from my dick. Nothing. It's not her. It's not the way she kisses. I rip our mouths apart, holding mine like it betrayed me.

"Why'd you stop?" Grace leans forward, pressing her breasts together using the inside of her biceps, "You were just starting to make me —"

"I can't do this." I step back. "I want to use you so badly to drown my pain, but I can't." The rawness of my words surprises me.

She pops off the table. "Use me," her eyes plead, "I want you to use me."

"Grace, no, you don't. Don't ever let anyone use you." I shake my head in disbelief. Where is this girl's self-worth? Grabbing my blunt from behind her, I turn to leave.

"What the fuck, Jace? You're like seriously fucked up for that. You know you liked it. You wouldn't have made out with me for that long if you didn't. Fucking douchebag! You'll never get a girl if you keep—"

I keep walking away until her obnoxious voice fades away. I keep walking until I enter the dorm hall. I keep walking until I fucking forget about her.

Fucking Belle, fucking. Fuck. Fuck. FUCK. There's no distraction for me, no escape. I try to drink, I think about Belle. I try to smoke. I definitely think about Belle. I try to hook up with some hot blonde with big tits, and all I can fucking think about is how I wish it was Belle. Her lips, her tits, her waist, her voice.

CHAPTER TWENTY
Marabelle

"Yo Belle, how's that play thing been?" Joey asks.

I feel like it's been a while since I've spent time solely with the boys. It's usually the six of us. I've seen them in school and stuff, but it hasn't been the three of us in a while.

Every group of six has its divisions of three. I'm a part of these three. I feel closer to Brandon and Joey than I do to the girls. We've all gone to school together since we were in Kindergarten, but somehow Brandon, Joey, and I have naturally gravitated toward each other. They're goofy and charming. I share some of my favorite memories with them.

I asked them to hang out after school today. This is one of the rare days that I don't have rehearsal after school, so I figured I should take advantage and do something else to distract my brain. It's been hard hanging around the girls after that night. My mind won't even take me back to Elena's sleepover, when we all found out. They all know, but no one asks. Elena has to be keeping them in the loop, but I don't even tell her much. The energy feels different whenever I'm around them lately; it's like they're walking on eggshells around me, scared I might crack.

My guts are spread out. I've already been cracked.

"Oh yeah, I forgot you're doing that nerd play," Brandon laughs.

"I never thought I would say this, but it's really fun. I get to pretend to be someone else, and it's so crazy because you really start to feel like the character when you're playing them."

"That's sick as fuck," Joey nods along. "We're coming to the play opening night. We were saying the other day how excited we are to see you."

"And *Freaky Friday* is a fantastic movie, so that's the only reason I'm going," Brandon says sarcastically.

"Oh, shut up!" I slap his arm next to me.

We got some lunch on our way home, and I'm driving them back to Brandon's house now. "What time are they coming over?" I ask.

"Elena texted me they'll be there in like 20." Joey passes his vape up to Brandon in the front seat. "You sure you don't want to stay, Belle, even for a little?"

"Yeah, no, I'm good. I have a ton of homework to catch up on, so—"

"Well, that's a lie," Brandon interrupts.

"A lie?" My pitch increases. "Really, guys?"

"Just tell us, Belle."

My heart fucking drops, and I slam on the breaks. All of our seat belts lock, jerking our heads forward.

"Jesus fucking Christ, are you trying to kill us?" Joey screams.

"GO. GO GO! You're stopped in the middle of the intersection," Brandon reaches out, grabbing the steering wheel from me. He doesn't move it.

The motion alone alerts me enough to snap me out of it.

"Oops," I giggle. "Sorry about that."

"Damn, I didn't think the fight was that bad, but it must be. You almost killed us Belle. "

"Wait," I look over to Brandon, "What fight?"

"Between you and the girls." He responds.

"We've noticed tensions have been high between you guys, so we assumed you got into a fight with them. " Joey says clarifying.

"Ooh. Um." I pull up to Brandon's house and put the car in the park. I should go along with whatever they think is happening between us. They could bring it up to the girls, though, and then I might be fucked. I remind myself how long I've been friends with these boys. As much as they care about me, they do not care about drama. They're boys. They want to know that there's no beef moving forward and that'll be that.

I choose to lie. "It was a stupid fight. Madison said something about Jace and I," I stutter, "I might have overreacted."

"So everyone took Ms. Perfect's side?" Joey asks.

"Yeah. I mean to be fair, I did call her a brainless whore." I throw up air quotes for some extra pizazz.

Brandon starts cracking up. "No way?"

"I mean, you're not wrong." Joey adds, "I'm sure she deserved it."

Joey isn't too fond of Madison. They clash a lot because of their difference in political views. That and the fact that sometimes, when we get drunk, they secretly make out. Madison has never admitted it to me, but I've gotten it out of Joey once or twice. They have that whole "mean to your crush" sort of thing going on, and they both feel weird about it because it goes against their beliefs. There's no need for me to bring it up right now because this is already working in my favor.

"Yeah, so I guess it's just been a little awkward since then," I confess.

Brandon isn't totally convinced. "What did Madison say about Jace? Because I feel like they always say bad shit about him," Brandon presses. "How is Jace anyway? When's the last time you guys spoke?"

"I'm not sure how Jace is," I ignore the first part of the question. "I haven't heard from him much."

I haven't heard from Jace much, that is since our very awkward conversation about my almost abortion. I have no idea what is happening between us. I know we called things off before I found out I was pregnant but I thought he loved me. It had only been a couple of days between then. A couple of days for him to completely fall out of love with me and not give a fuck that I'm pregnant. It makes no sense.

"Ah, hello," Brandon waves his hand in front of my face, "Earth to Belle."

"Jeez, Belle, if you keep picking at that, the whole thing is going to unravel."

I look down and observe what my hands started doing that my mind lost control of. I've picked at the lacing of my steering wheel. Jagged and rough, I guess my care for my Chevy went out the fucking window. I love this car. I spend most of my time in my car. My car brings deep comfort when nothing else can nowadays. It's my force field. I cannot believe I hurt my baby.

"Belle, seriously, stop." I feel Joey's warm hand make contact with my shoulder. "Maybe you smoked a little too much before."

We all start laughing to fizzle out whatever the hell they've witnessed. I have to keep reminding myself that they're boys, and the furthest they read into things is whether they could take on a bear or not.

Brandon and Joey collect their things before shuffling out of the car.

"Bye guys I'll see you tomorrow."

"See you tomorrow, Belles."

"Thanks for the ride," Joey calls out. And they're both gone.

I called four different abortion clinics. I spoke to each representative about their availability and the severity of my situation. They all expressed their sympathy as they told me the next available appointments. Nothing was available soon. So I wait.

4 weeks

28 days

672 hours

40,320 minutes I wait until my appointment.

Living in New Jersey has been a blessing. I was grateful that I could get an abortion without having to go out of state. I couldn't even fathom the thought if I had to do that. It's hard enough to sneak out of the house to get to the doctor. How would I do it if I had to travel far for it?

When I booked my appointment, they told me that I'd have to come back a couple of weeks after the procedure to make sure everything worked and that everything was gone.

I want everything to be gone.

I always knew my access to abortion was legal in my home state, but I had no idea how hard it was to get one done. Our sex ed in school was a complete joke. The only thing I got out of sex-ed was how to properly disrupt a class to our very unqualified, pervy gym teacher.

My opinion on abortion was always clear. It should be the women's choice, no questions asked. Regardless of her reasoning, or situation, it is her body and her decision what she does with it. I still feel that way, but it's much harder when it's actually happening to you. Both choices are hard for a woman. Abortion is not to be taken lightly. My heart breaks for every single name listed in the appointment book. Are they all just waiting? Walking around this world knowing their impending doom?

CHAPTER TWENTY-ONE

I have the period app on my phone. I've had it on my phone for a couple of years now. I like it because I know when my period is coming. I was never too strict about using it, but when I remembered, I would log my period and the occasional symptoms. Sometimes, life happens, and you forget what day you started your last period.

    I logged that I'm pregnant in the app. I made the mistake of logging that I'm pregnant in the app. It changed the whole layout. I wanted to make more sense of when it happened, trying to retrace my last inputted data with my current situation.

Jace was right. I don't always take my pill on time every single day. Sometimes, I miss it by a couple of minutes or so. I'm not even sure if that affects anything. I guess it doesn't matter now because I'm pregnant, and the birth control didn't control shit.

A tiny dinosaur-looking thing advances week by week on this app, showing me a visual representation of what is happening inside my belly.

It's week 8.

I am not okay.

I puked when I got home today. All over my bed, all over my hands, all over my phone. I couldn't control it. I have become addicted to looking at the dinosaur. It morphs and mutates, growing its humanity day by day. I go to school, I laugh with my friends, I become Tess Coleman, I come home. Everyday. While this thing lives, breaths, grows, inside me.

This app is a blade. I am cutting over and over again. It agonizes, but I can't stop. I like the pain too much. At least it lets me feel something.

anything…

Jace has been given the whole rundown. He knows when the appointment is for. He knows that gave me plenty of time to deposit the money to give to Elena without it looking suspicious. I took two hundred dollars out at first and then a hundred each the last two weeks. My mom hasn't said a thing. He's still saying he'll get me the money, but I know he won't. We talk here and there. We talk laconically. I've hinted that I'm struggling, but he never takes the bait. I want him here. I need some support. I can't walk around every day knowing what is going on inside me. He's the only other one who knows. I thought maybe he could understand a fraction of what I feel like.

Jace doesn't care to.

If he wanted to be a part of this, he would be. Sometimes he'll text me back just to say some fucked up shit. He keeps calling it a baby. For god sake, it's not a baby, and it isn't going to be one. It's like he's made it his mission to make me feel guilty. How about I feel guilty enough, Jace? I know what it looks like at 5 weeks, 6 weeks, 7 weeks, 8 weeks. I'll know what it feels like to have something and to no longer.

My brain has become a perfectly divided pie graph. It is split into three sections. The fact that I'm pregnant, the play, and Nick. I try to focus on Nick, on that night we spent together. It feels like it was years ago, another lifetime even. To lay there with him made me feel seen. I can't help but feel like if Nick accidentally got me pregnant, he would treat me with grace. It's a scary situation for anyone, but Nick seems like he's good in a crisis.

I came to the open gym today. Nick and I have made indirect eye contact across the way a couple of times. We're exchanging glances when the other is not looking, being very careful not to get caught. I can feel his eyes on me, so you have to be quick with it. We've been at it since I walked in.

"Marabelle," Nick taps on the glass of my car window.

I jump, adrenaline flooding my body. How long has he been standing there?

I look down at my hands to see what they've done again. The leather of my steering wheel has been torn to bits at this point. I get put in these trances where I lose complete control of my body.

My mind goes and goes and goes, and my hands need something to tear apart. I think I really want to tear myself apart. But that would be too messy, too bloody, and a very gruesome suicide.

I roll down my window, a smile forming on my face. "Nick, hey, what are you doing out here?"

"I saw you head out for the night. I didn't get a chance to say hi."

"Oh, right, I'm sorry." And my smile disappears.

"No, no, it's okay. I haven't talked to you much since we hooked up." He places his hand on the lip of the windowsill. "I feel like you're kind of avoiding me, Belle."

My thumbs circle his pinky nail, "Green checkered. Hmm, I like it."

"Yeah, don't worry, no more freaky impostor parties coming up. I just liked the design." He says, leaning into my touch.

"Good cause I can't handle any more of those."

I break the connection, looking up into his eyes; I can't drag this man down with me. I don't deserve him. I'm not ready for someone like him.

I'm confused and hormonal. I shouldn't be near Nick like this.

"Marabelle," Nick reaches for my hand again, "Why have you been avoiding me?"

"Remember what you said the night of the party? To let you know when I'm ready for boys to stop treating me like shit?"

He nods.

"Well, I'm not ready yet, Nick. I have a particular asshole in my life that I'm still dealing with, and it wouldn't be fair to entertain the both of you." That's not completely false. I don't want to lie to Nick, but the truth isn't something I'm capable of right now.

"Yup." He bows his head in one fluid motion, "I understand."

"That night meant more to me than I'll ever admit to anyone," I express.

"Fuck Marabelle," Nick drops my hand, "It's frustrating that you can't see your own worth. You should be able to admit to everyone how fucking amazing that night was, how amazing all of our nights are. You should be able to own your feelings. And whatever particular asshole you can't let go of is going to bring you both down with him." He steps back from my car. His hands are the last to let go. "I won't play these games with you, Belle."

"Nick, wait. I'm sorry. This is all just too much for me."

He turns to walk away. I want to run out of this car. I want so fucking badly to ask him to hold me until this feeling inside me escapes, but I sit there. Frozen. Choking on my tears. The window rolls up as I stare forward blankly. One motion is followed by the next, and my body moves for me. I scream as loud as I fucking can, banging on the steering wheel like it's my face in front of me.

How did I get here?

How am I pregnant?

How do I get out of here?

Act III

CHAPTER TWENTY-TWO
Jace

I have a long walk from my last lecture hall to the student center where I tutor. It's end to end on the campus, so I tuck my earbuds in and begin my journey. It's slowly starting to get warmer out. The end of March is one of my favorite times of the year. I can get away with a flannel and sweatpants and be perfectly comfortable. I also love baseball season. That's the only way my father and I bond. The wind picks up the faster I walk, bouncing through my tawny hair. I try really hard not to think about Belle, but somehow, my mind always makes room for her.

Did you go? I text Belle.

Belle: Wednesday 8:30, an estimated price of $520.

Me: Oh, ok.

Belle: Why

Me: Just asking.

That's all I say.

She sent me the same response a couple of weeks ago, but I wanted to talk to her. I didn't know what to say or how to say it, so I thought that was my best option. I've never been particularly good with my emotions. Emotions are for the weak, and I'm not weak. I will not coddle with Belle. I will not be all mushy with her like she can't handle this. That's not who I am. That's not who I'll ever be. She's always been trying to get something out of me as long as I've known her. I'll admit I've had a few slip-ups and some breakdowns here and there; I know she holds onto those. She uses them to remind her that I'm human. Uses them to prove that the love I have for her is real.

Belle's been on the character list of my life forever. We've grown up in the same town alongside one another. She was someone I crushed on as a kid and knew I would crush on even harder by the time high school rolled around.

There was one night when everything changed for me. I had some stuff going on with my family, and I did what any typical teenager would do: I went to a party. As soon as I walked in, I knew I shouldn't be there. I wasn't in the right head space and couldn't talk about it with any of my friends. I slipped into one of the rooms off of the kitchen to make myself a drink and take a beat. I had let some tears shed, hoping that the rest of my pain would subside so I could enjoy the party. I was the party, I couldn't be crying away like some little bitch.

Belle came tumbling in a couple of minutes later. I was surprised to see her because she was a grade younger than me. Belle always had her way with people. She was intoxicating. She hid her alcohol in the cabinet under me; smart girl. She acknowledged me but played it cool, pretending like she didn't see my swollen red eyes. Her finesse has always been so attractive to me. She fixed herself a drink and came to stand in front of me. She ever so gently wiped my tears with her soft, delicate fingers. She held me there for a while, and I broke. Our mutual crush transformed that night. It was the first time I ever broke in front of someone else. I told her my parents were separating and how fucking tense the house was. The ventilation in our house ran on fumes of violence. She let me feel, let me cry and then turned it around and made me smile. From that night on, Belle has had my heart.

I press the bar on the door and push forward as I enter the student center. I took up extra shifts to stack my money. I will pay Belle back, but it's taking some time. Tuition was due at the beginning of the semester, the same time I found out about the pregnancy, so things are tight. Money, money, money is all I can see now. I pay for everything myself: my car, insurance, gas, food, school, everything.

My Mom believes in independence. She thought college was a waste of time, so if I wanted to go, I had to pay for it myself. I respect her beliefs, because they have made me a stronger man. I have set up my future, so I never have to worry about money. That's all my parents would fucking fight about. If that means grinding it all out and being miserable for a little while, then so be it. I'm going to school, so money isn't a concern for me in the future. I'm a natural leader so I know one day I'll run a business that can get me closer to my end goal. I have to meet that end goal.

I'm on a partial academic scholarship, which honestly doesn't help much. I have to work for my money, which is always at the forefront of my mind. Now, I have to work for my money on top of the six hundred dollars I owe to Belle. There's a lot on my back. The weight just keeps getting heavier and heavier.

Marabelle

It's all over my hands. They're stuck together by the thick white cream. I finally got my sesame seed bagel with hot sauce and cream cheese. Why do bagel stores pack on this much cream cheese? They put way too much stuff on it. It makes it impossible to eat without half of it oozing out the back and making a mess. I keep squeezing the excess out, creating a mini mountain in the foil on my lap. I would be gagging at what I'm consuming at any other time, but I'm relishing it today.

"I'm glad I got bagels. You need to eat before this," Elena slurps her iced coffee.

"It's not like I don't eat. I eat too much. I want everything," I flick the last glop of smear off my bagel. "Thank you, though, for everything."

"Of course, Belle."

Taylor Swift's voice is what gets us to the doctor's office in peace. She has such a way with her words. I wish I could express this feeling inside me as well as she does.

Elena didn't ask too much, she knows what's about to happen. This is for real this time. She has to be as uncomfortable as I am.

Would if he was here? Would he be able to sit here in this waiting room by my side? He was able to be inside me, perhaps for a little too long, but he can't be here today. He can't even offer a text message. Is he thinking about me? Would I want him here? Do I want him to know how cold it is in the office or how fucking distant you have to put your consciousness from your own body in order to make it through?

I came all the way up here to observe and watch this fucked up show.

The young girl makes her way into the office. She sat in the waiting room for eighteen minutes. She gets checked by three doctors before being escorted to the final room. She takes a seat on the crinkly white paper. They ask her questions; they poke her veins, and they double-check that this is exactly what she wants to be doing. They ask her eight different times if she's sure she wants to proceed.

She says yes every time, losing grit with her tone.

The final doctor walks in. He's a man. The only man she's seen in this building so far. All the women who work under him must not be qualified for the job. The sad truth is they're probably more qualified for the job. That's just what happens when the world operates under a patriarchy.

Men get women pregnant.

Men have the power to administer the abortion.

Men have the final say on whether our whole country should be allowed to have a choice.

The man doctor explains what is going to happen. The young girl doesn't hear a word he says. She is terrified.

Luckily for her, I listened. He told her there's eleven pills she is going to take. The first one, he hands it to her, is to be taken now. She swallows and places the white Dixie cup down. The next ten will be inserted into the vagina 24-48 hours after our appointment. This, he says, holding up a five-inch needle will stop the fetus from growing. The pills to follow will allow your body to pass the pregnancy naturally.

He motions her to lie down on the bed. She didn't need to put on a gown; she had already done that in the other rooms. They checked her again with that gigantic cold wand. They told her she was 8 weeks, 3 days.

She moves her head around the room to try and find something to focus on to ease the discomfort. The male doctor injects the needle into her hip before she can brace herself. I begin to fall back into her body but don't quite make it. He explains it may cause some numbing but that is totally normal. He asks her if she has any questions, to which she shakes her head no. Aimlessly, I follow Belle's body all the way back home. I try to reenter her again but she won't let me in. She doesn't want to feel her consciousness right now.

    She doesn't want to feel anything.

CHAPTER TWENTY-THREE

8 weeks 3 days.

These five pills are staring back at me. I imagine them as the devil's disciples. That's what this is: dark, foreign energy. I don't know much of what happened today, but I'm still trying to wrap my head around the whole thing. I left because I couldn't handle it. Now that I need to know what the fuck to do with these pills, I had no choice but to come back. I have begun a toxic relationship with my mind and body. Leaving and coming back and leaving and coming back. Exactly what I do with Jace.

Jace.

He got me here. He did this to me. He's the reason I'm hanging out with the devil.

I loathe him. I want every single bad thing to happen to him. How could he be so unaffected by all of this? How could I be so stupid to let him back in again? I said goodbye to him before auditioning for the play; I should've stuck to that. I hoped this year would be different for us. He brought me those pathetic flowers paired with a pathetic apology. Actually, I don't even recall him saying the words I'm sorry. I fucking melted, fell for the manipulating love I'm addicted to receiving. That should've been my final straw. He only came back to have his way with me. He wanted it to be on his terms, under his control. He's a coward who claimed he was a lion—stupid girl.

Round and round, I kept falling for it. The night of Madison's party…that had to be when this happened. One night. One stupid, weak night where all we wanted was to be in each other's arms.

HOW IS THAT STILL ALL I WANT?

After everything he's done to me.

I shimmy my sweats down, exposing my hip. I press around it to feel what they did to me. It's hard to the touch. I get closer to the mirror, looking to see if I can find the indentation from the needle. It looks like nothing happened, but it doesn't feel like that.

I couldn't sleep on my left side all night and day. I guess. What time is it? I missed school. Okay, at least today's Friday so the weekend will help with my forced absences. My Mom has always left for work before I go to school; it's always worked out in my favor. I'm particularly grateful for the timing through all of this. What she doesn't know won't hurt her.

If my Mom knew her daughter skipped school yesterday to get an abortion, she might have a heart attack. She can never know. Nobody can ever know. I will die with this. Take this to my grave. This will be my deepest, darkest secret.

It's somewhere between the 24-48 hour mark. My consciousness, rejoining my body, has allowed me to make sense of what to do with these five pills. I've created a tight funnel, only allowing basic necessities to keep me afloat. I was told to insert these pills into my vagina. The pills are sealed in the package in rows of 4-3-2-1, creating a triangle shape.

Insert the first four pills and wait twelve hours. Then insert the next three pills, wait another twelve hours, and blah blah blah.

I overlap my thumbs on the plastic side of the foil, pushing forward to pop each pill out. I place them on my countertop next to my bathroom sink. The chalky white color rubs off from the heat of my fingers. So, this stopped the fetus from growing. I retrace my bare thigh. And these, I sweep the pills into the cup of my hand, will allow it to pass through me.

I remove my pants all the way and pee. Standing bare in front of my mirror, my hands wrap over my belly.

I don't think I fully understood how humans came to be until this happened. So much more goes into it than sex. My hands soothe the area, offering a brief sense of sorrow before squatting to hover the ground. I thought this position would be best because this is how I learned to put a tampon in. The first time you go to put a tampon in, you can't comprehend how something so foreign is supposed to get shoved into your body. When you find the right angle, it just does. I thought this would be the right angle. I grab one pill beginning to insert it into my vagina.

Did they say how far it's supposed to go in?

I can't remember that part; I'm assuming pretty far, though, so it dissolves. I'm able to get the first pill in, and I audibly exhale a sigh of relief. The pressure of all of this is starting to ease the quicker I get through all these steps. I reach the top of the counter to grab the second and third pills. I drop one straight onto the blue fuzzy bathmat under me. My hands graze through the fur, trying to find where the damn pill went.

Would if I miss one pill? Would if I'm not doing this right? Will it still work if I'm one pill short? How much time can pass before inserting the next pill? I have to find that pill, or I'm going to be fucked.

I'm on my hands and knees searching for it like my life depends on it. My life does depend on it.

"Belle's," I hear my sister calling my name. I don't answer, waiting to see if she'll leave it. I'll pretend I'm sleeping.

"Belle, Belle, Belle," she continues, "I want to show you a new number we learned today. Are you awake?"

My poor sister has no idea what I'm doing behind these doors. No one knows what I'm going through. Tears begin to fall down my cheeks, as I've torn this rug apart, looking for the pill.

I disguise my voice, sit back on my heels, and say, "Hey, Linds, give me a couple minutes. I'll be right down to see."

"Okie dokie."

I find the pill wedged between the seal on my counter and the floor vent. I grab the winning lottery ticket. I don't know what I would've done if this thing fell through those cracks. The pills are tiny, a little bigger than a tick-tack. It was millimeters away from going down that vent.

"Thank you," I say out loud and insert it inside the same way I did the other. I can feel the first pill already starting to dissolve. I'm in and out with the last ones as fast as possible. I don't want to know what's going on in there. Get in and get out.

They sent me home with a couple of maxi pads and a bunch of paperwork. The paperwork is a copy of my record that I was there, as well as a list of side effects from the pills. I place one of the maxi pads on my underwear and get changed. They said I could bleed for up to a week; "it will be like a more intense period." I flashed into the memory of those words relayed to me by the man. A maxi pad will do, I guess.

I make my way downstairs, grabbing my favorite spot on the couch. Lindsay comes running from the kitchen immediately pushing the tables to the side closet to the windows to make room for her demonstration. I cozy up in the L of the couch, wrapping a knitted green blanket over my body.

"Since we have nationals coming up after Easter, our coaches wanted to change up one of our routines," Lindsay stands in the center of the room, "And guess what Belle?"

"What?"

"They're giving me a solo!" She screams.

"OMG, Lindsay, that's amazing! At nationals, too, that's huge."

"I know I'm like so good they couldn't resist," she says as she flips her hair with sass.

I smile, appreciating her comedic relief. She never fails to bring me peace.

"Alright, so let me show you what we started today."

She begins the choreography. We discuss it, I give her encouragement. I can't entirely give her tips because she's always had me beat in the dancing department. That's why we're such a good team for our family performances. I did the singing, she did the dancing, and together, it was Alervez sister perfection.

Sitting on this couch watching my sister is making me emotional. I hope someday, if I do decide to have children, I get to watch them put on little shows like this. I did it as a girl; my sister does it, and now I can understand why it brought my mother so much joy—purely innocent childhood fun.

I will never have any children. I don't deserve to. How can I choose to take one life just to turn around and embrace another? It's not right. It wouldn't be fair.

"I think you're going to kill it, Linds." She spins into a pirouette.

"I agree. I already have down most of the choreography," she says.

"Yeah, for just learning them today, they look great."

Keys rattle through the mudroom, and my Mom appears from the garage door.

"Hi, girls. Dad should be home any minute, and then we're going to head out," she drops all the stuff her arms were holding onto the table in front of her.

I totally forgot they're leaving tonight for our annual family Easter trip.

My Mom continues, "I hope you packed after dance, Lindsay. That's why I dropped you off," she gives her a tight look.

"Yes, Mom, I packed; I have my toothbrush left to grab."

"Okay, sweetie, well then, let's get to it."

My sister skips off to probably go back all of her things. I join the conversation I'm intentionally not being included in, "Where's Dad?"

"He got held up at work. I got you some groceries in case you need anything while we're gone." She slams the cans of soup down on the table. "You know, Belle, I'm really disappointed you're not coming this weekend. You're going to spend Easter all alone?"

"Mom, I'm an adult. I'll be fine. I have rehearsal almost every day anyway, so I'll be busy." That's a lie. We only had rehearsal—right now. We have rehearsal right now that I'm obviously missing.

"Yeah, I know, but it won't be the same without you."

I can't stand the look in her eyes. I need to get out of here. I pretend my phone is ringing and quickly grab it from my pocket. "Sorry, Ma Elena is calling me. Have to take this. Love you, see you Monday!" I march up the steps. I feel guilty, but I have to be selfish. I can't talk to my Mom when I know what I've done.

My Mom is cool. She's never been too overbearing or too parenty. I respect her and know her rules, but I also know she's a bit naive. Especially having Lindsay as my younger sister, she's distracted sometimes with her responsibilities towards her. My hyper-independence leads my Mom to believe I don't need her.

I need her right now.

I go to the bathroom to pee and to check this pad. I felt the blood begin when I was watching Lindsay.

The damage on the pad doesn't alarm me compared to how my stomach is feeling. My blood looks dark. There's barely any trace of red. The amount checks out with what day one of my period looks like.

I'm beginning to get cold, very, very cold. I nuzzle into my bed and turn on Love Island. I get washed away into an ocean of waves.

CHAPTER TWENTY-FOUR

pain.

CHAPTER TWENTY-FIVE

This wave is enormous. I have butterflies in my stomach the closer it gets to me. It's scaling me, determining if I'm strong enough to take on its mighty force. The waves decide there is no room for mercy. I hold my breath and brace myself to go under. I am tumbling in a storm of pain. I'm bleeding like I have never bled in my life. It keeps coming and coming. I try to come up for air, but the next wave takes me under, bigger and more ruthless. My insides feel like they are being individually shredded by cat claws. Plucked, ripped, and torn apart.

I have been in the same position for hours. I thought my body would shut down at a certain point. Allow me to sleep through the agony. The agony wants to be felt. I am supposed to feel each and every pinch, squeeze, and contraction in order to understand exactly what I have begun.

There is no going back.

I debated not taking the last set of pills. I can't stand this feeling anymore. I hold my stomach. It makes it worse. I dig my fingernails into my thighs so hard I break skin. I am trying to feel pain anywhere else in my body to redirect its energy. It is a force that will not be reckoned with.

It takes 24 minutes to soak through a pad. I ran out of those bullshit maxi pads they sent me home with fast. I had to raid my Mom's stuff. I typically use tampons and panty liners, so I didn't have any three-inch thick cotton lying around. I found a box in her bathroom. They look super old, but I made it work. I have no strength to go to the store and buy more. I could barely make it out of bed to get these.

I think I might die up here. It would take hours, maybe even days, before someone found my decaying body. Maybe the smell would be able to signal something's wrong. I imagine I would be surrounded in my cold blood. My womb at the center, circling the circumference of my body. I'm hunched in fetal position; in my dying moments, I attempt to bring comfort to myself.

There's not much of any fetal positioning happening inside me. I pass clots of blood with each pad I throw away. I was dissecting them at first, scared by what I saw coming out of me. Thick and hard chunks of blood scattered throughout the pad. The blood was the home base for those pieces.

I can't look anymore. I'm trying to remove myself from what is happening, but I'm afraid my body won't let me fully leave because we have shifted into survival mode. Fight or flight, but flight isn't an option.

I haven't heard from anyone. Not my friends, not Nick, and definitely not Jace.

It's been a constant dance between my bed and bathroom. Those are the only places I can focus on right now. I clutch my knees tighter into my chest. This position seems to be the only one that doesn't make death seem desirable. I try to think of something, anything other than the pain. I can not.

So I pray.

I used to believe in God when I was a child. I grew up in the Catholic church following my mother and father's wishes. I was baptized and made communion, even confirmation, but it never resonated with me. I have always been fascinated by all of the different religions. I didn't feel like I belonged to just one. As I got older, I didn't agree with a lot of the rules Catholicism seemed to push. Ironically, abortion being the biggest one. Maybe I have sinned, and this is my punishment.

I close my eyes, asking God to offer me grace:

I don't know how this prayer thing works or if I'm doing it right, but I really need you right now, God. I know I'm not supposed to ask for things only when I need them but this is too much for me. I didn't mean to get pregnant. I wanted to be free this year. Why am I being punished like this? Do you understand why I had to do this, God? I can't have a baby right now. I'm only eighteen. I'm still in high school. I have no money for a child, nor do I have the mental capability to raise one. I have an absent partner. Will you forgive me? This is all really terrifying and I'm feeling so incredibly alone. If you're listening God, please help me.

CHAPTER TWENTY-SIX
The American Nightmare

The leaves are beginning to change shades. I take this walk most days to get out of the house a little. I've been feeling lost within myself, constantly worrying about what everyone else needs around me. I guess that's a trait of all mothers. We settled into our new apartment a couple of weeks ago. It's a piece of shit, above a bakery that we grew up going to in our small town. It's all we could afford. At least the crumb cake is good.

I carry the stroller up the steep narrow steps. I'm welcomed by paint peeling off the door, and a stoop too small to balance the stroller, myself, and the baby. I fiddle with the keys that insist on getting jammed every single time we open the door. My arms are losing strength holding the baby. On my third try, were in. Stepping inside the apartment I let out a deep breath.

"Hi! A little help."

As if he couldn't hear me coming up the stairs, or struggling to get in for five minutes, Jace comes to grab the baby from my arms, kissing his forehead and placing him down in his playpen. I nudge the stroller into the corner of our living room and remove my jacket. This is the best spot we could find for it, shoved into the corner of our already crammed space.

Moments pass without words. I decide to speak first. "Doesn't he look cute with these little beanies?" I ask. Our neutral ground is the baby.

Jace hasn't put his phone down since the moment we walked through the door. He glances up from his phone briefly to say, "Yeah."

I take it work didn't go so well today. I don't want to pry because I know how he gets when I pry. I always ask him how his day was or what he wants for dinner but it's bleak.

"I think I'm going to pick a couple more up from the store next time I go," I continue.

He doesn't respond. Jace is under a lot of pressure. He's working full-time for his Uncle's electrician company, and I appreciate what he reluctantly had to do but I don't know how else I can be supportive.

I was home with him through the first months of my postpartum, so I couldn't work. We've discussed it's not worth it to put our son in daycare while we both work. We would be losing money. Daycare prices do not correlate with minimum wage. It's way harder than you even expect it to be when you decide to go through with it.

I start to prepare dinner while Jace goes to shower. He spends a lot of time in the shower after work. There was a time after the baby was born that I could've sworn I heard him crying in there. I never brought it up, I don't bring many things up to him. I think about it all the time though. We try to argue as least as possible for the sake of our child. I think we silently agreed to do so by tip-toeing around each other.

The steam from the bubbling water burns my hand as I toss the pasta inside. I've learned more about cooking than I ever have in my life. It's not like I didn't know how to prepare food for myself before, but that's all it was, preparing the food. If Mom was working late or I needed to eat before play rehearsal I could figure out how to put things together to make a decent meal. Now, I have to feed my family, every day.

I'm no cook by any means, but I try to follow some recipes on YouTube to make things half edible. Most of the time when it sucks, Jace will go out and grab McDonald's or something for us. He's never ridiculed me for any of it, but I know deep down he gets frustrated. It's the passive-aggressive huffs and puffs that signify it. How can I blame him, who wouldn't want to come home from work to a meal already prepared, and a happy little wife?

That's not reality. I feel like I'm living inside of the American nightmare. Have the baby because it's the right thing to do. Have the baby because there's no other choice. Let the man be the breadwinner. Cook for him. Clean for him. And make sure your primary focus is the baby. Actually, make sure you're so hyper-focused on the baby that you lose yourself in the process.

Home

I feel his warm hand come around my body, pulling me closer to his chest. He hugs my breasts placing a lazy kiss on the back of my shoulder. I love the weekend mornings we get to have together. I could twist in these sheets with him for hours. I let the moment consume me, grateful for what we've built out of a shit situation. Not every moment is easy, and we've both had to sacrifice a lot, but it's all worth it.

I roll over facing his sleepy eyes. We wrap limb by limb in the position we cherish so dearly. I run my hand through his knotty hair.

"Is he awake yet?" Jace mumbles.

"No," I whisper, "are you awake yet."

"No, not awake yet."

I delicately trace my fingers in all the places he loves to be touched. Behind his ear, down the side of his neck, lapping circles over his back, all the way to the crevice of his hips. His skin is so soft there. It's like baby skin that never matured.

"Mmm." He moans into my touch. He knows exactly what I'm trying to do, and we do it.

Jace knows me better than any else does. No matter where we are, we are each other's home. I go to grab the baby, waking him for his first feed of the day. Jace freshens up in the shower first because he offered to do the grocery shopping today. A fair compromise.

I think my Mom is coming over later to spend some time with her grandson, and her daughter of course. She has been more than helpful since I had the baby. She offered to pay the first three months of rent in our new apartment until we were able to get our feet off the ground.

The apartment isn't luxury, but it's good enough for our little family for now. Jace works full-time for his Uncle's electrician company which he doesn't totally hate. I haven't been focusing on work, just taking care of my son and figuring out how this whole parenting thing works. I want to ask my Mom today what she thinks about me starting online classes for college.

I was doing some research and saw that I would be able to go on financial aid due to our situation. My Mom watches the baby all the time when we ask so I don't presume it will be a problem on the days I need her to. Like when I have an exam or something.

I want to go back to school. I never finished my senior year in person. I was able to shift to online courses for the last three months of my senior year. I quit the play, I couldn't stomach the thought of seeing all my peers while everyone knew I was pregnant. That and my belly would have been impossible to hide on stage. My friends were never directly not supportive but I mean an eighteen-year-old having a baby is never sunshine and rainbows.

I really only talk to Elena, Joey, and Brandon now. Madison and Kelly come around sometimes but they don't show much interest. To be fair, they both go to college in Delaware, and I'm sure their friend with a baby isn't at the forefront of their minds. Elena FaceTime's me from FIT in New York a couple of times a week, and Brandon and Joey go to community college not far from our hometown. I see them the most often.

It's crazy to see how much has happened. I had to change so fast, down a trajectory that was so different from everyone else's. I think if I do start taking classes online then I'll be able to work part-time somewhere. Jace told me I don't have to work right now, that we're doing okay with his income. Truthfully I don't want to have to rely on my Mom at all for any help. The older we get the less mercy the world gives us for being teen parents.

The moments of darkness are worth it to us. Our baby boy makes us happier than anything. He is my heart, my world. He looks just like his Daddy. None of my genes carried over to him. He's the perfect blonde-haired, blue-eyed baby. His mannerisms mirror mine more than anything. He's very expressive with his face, which keeps us very entertained. All the sacrifices, heartache, and pain endured for this baby to be born has brought Jace and I closer than ever. He was a blessing.

"I'm heading to the grocery store now," Jace places a kiss on my forehead, "I'll be home later." He goes to kiss our son in the same spot. "I love you guys."

Double-Edged Sword

I go around turning on all the lights. I lift the blinds above his bed. The sunlight floods the dungeon, emphasizing the mess that surrounds me. I pick up dirty clothes and throw them in the laundry basket. I throw away old food and a dozen empty soda bottles. There's bits of weed scattered around his grinder. This shit is disgusting. I'm tired of cleaning his mess up.

He left his phone on the charger while he showers, he never does that. I'm so tempted to look at it. He's been pretty lovey with me recently and I know that means he's up to something. His affection towards me is hot and cold. His affection with the baby is constant.

Our baby is his world, he adores that kid more than I've ever seen him adore anything. Sometimes I try not to get jealous with the amount of attention he gives the baby over me. I gave him that baby. I gave up everything to have that baby. It might be selfish of me to feel this way, but I can't help but feel it. He only shows me affection when it's convenient for him. Then and only then do we get to play house and be one big happy family. But most of the time I'm waiting to see what mood he'll be in that day.

We're not together. We're co-existing, co-parenting. I never asked to be together. I asked that if we are going to have a baby that I have unconditional support.

I tap the screen on his phone. I hold my breath anticipating the trauma. There's a SnapChat from Grace. My heart drops. I've seen her name on his phone before. I've nearly ripped my eyes out of their socket to peek at his screen. I've brought it up to him before. He's dismissed it as an old friend from college who he keeps in touch with. I pushed for more information, I know what he does when I have the baby at my Mom's house, but he's never admitted it. I can guarantee Grace is a massive part of those nights. We fight over it constantly, but the behavior never stops.

I'm trapped, I can't leave, I can't complain, I can't force his love. My eyes are locked on her name. Does she know he has a baby? I choose not to pick a fight with him today, we're supposed to spend the day together, all three of us. I slide my pointer finger over and lock his phone until the display of her name fades to black.

In the beginning, Jace was adamant about me getting an abortion, he basically pushed it on me. Eventually, he did a 180. He totally changed his mind and was willing to sacrifice pursuing his college degree to go work full-time. And that's what we did.

It's not ideal. We live in the basement of his parents home. I take turns going back and forth from his house to mine, but we spend the most time together at his. I don't fully trust him when I have to leave the baby alone with him or his Mom. I feel very protective over my creation, even when it comes to sharing him with Jace. I don't agree with a lot of Jace's Mom's parenting style. We've gotten into fights about it before. It's his son, and he has a say in his life too, but for some reason, it feels like I should have more of a say for being his Mom.

It's very complicated between us. We have a family together so there's a sense of obligation to be together. We obviously love each other but fighting is our love language. Our stance on our relationship status is different every day. Every hour.

Sometimes I regret it. I wish I was strong enough to not have listened to everyone around me. His mother didn't believe abortion was an option, and once he told her, she made it her mission to talk me out of it. She called my Mom and told her I was pregnant. I didn't even get to tell my own mother. My Mom wasn't stoked about the whole abortion thing, but she did want it to be my choice. She likes Jace and saw that he was willing to make sacrifices to make this work. That was the leading contender in her evaluation. I know what choice I made, and I love my baby, but I don't love my life. It's fucked up to admit, but sometimes I wonder where I would be if I never had it.

CHAPTER TWENTY-SEVEN

Gasping for air, my eyes shoot open. I launch up, slapping a hand to my chest. It rises and falls sporadically, and I can feel my thick breath escaping my lungs. I look around, confused, trying to decipher where I am or what happened. I'm in my room; the sun is about to set, and I'm soaked. My body is sticky with sweat, and it feels like I've pissed the bed. I throw the sheets off of my waist, revealing my legs underneath. A giant puddle of blood surrounds my body.

Fuck.

How long have I been asleep? When did I fall asleep?

The pad in my underwear was fucking useless. I sit there frozen, dumbfounded by the amount of blood that has come out of me. I lightly lift each leg and stand to observe the damage. My underwear is ruined. My shorts are ruined. I lift my sheets. They're ruined. I lift my mattress pad, it's ruined. I lift and lift and lift, each layer of destruction making its way deeper and deeper, all the way down to the core.

Am I supposed to bleed this much?

I run to my bathroom, stripping myself of all my disgusting clothes. The coolness of the toilet seat attempts to settle my beating heart. I pee because I really don't know what else to do. I've never seen this much blood before. The blood must've been nonstop through my sleep. I took the last set of pills, so this has to be the bulk of it.

it.

I feel immediate release from between my legs. My butt has stamped the toilet seat with blood. I reach to flush, but the graphic contents inside the bowl alarm me. There's a golf ball size of something that has passed through me. It's bright red floating in the toilet water. Swirls disperse around the golf ball, creating tiny streams of diluted blood. I flush the toilet, holding down the handle to make sure it doesn't clog.

What the fuck is happening to me?

I check my phone to see if there are any texts from the outside world while turning my shower handle as hot as it will go.

Mom: Happy Easter, my baby girl! Love and miss you <3

Another message:

We're heading home tomorrow and should be home around 8 pm Monday night. I can't wait to squeeze you!

I respond:

Me: Sorry, I knocked out after rehearsal. Love you too, can't wait to see you <33

I'm running out of excuses. I'm running out of ways to distract my Mom from what is going on in her house. I wish she were home this weekend, maybe she would notice that something is off with me. I never ignore my Mom's texts that long; she has to think something is up with me. I wish she would ask me what's wrong so I could tell her. I need someone.

I always thought I would be better off alone. I honestly prefer to be alone. Sometimes at night, I would wish that I could be the only person on planet Earth so I wouldn't have to deal with anyone else. My own sanity is much more comforting than being surrounded by others. I'm a lost cause—a worthless, broken soul. Right now, all I want is a house full of noise. I want my family back. It's too quiet. I am left in my own company to finish the battle I began.

Be careful what you wish for.

My shower is dark, hot, and violent. I've been sitting on the floor of my shower, bleeding and crying and screaming. It hurts. I'm scared. Something doesn't feel right.

I rummage through the stack of papers with soaking wet hands. My eyes scan the pages, searching for side effects. The usual headache, nausea, twenty-item list is there. And then on one of the pages, it says: *Contact your doctor immediately if any of the following side effects occur:*

-Excessively heavy vaginal bleeding

-unusual tiredness or weakness

-dizziness

-vomiting

This has to just be a usual part of the process. I mean, the man did say it should be a more intense period, but this is like all the blood I've ever bled combined into one flow. I guess it's fine. I'm fine. I have to be fine.

I fixed myself some soup and took a box of crackers to my room. Warm food is helping. I'm starting to feel stronger and much better than when I woke up. I convince myself I'm strong enough to drive to the drugstore around the corner from my house. I'm running out of pads and need more immediately. What else am I supposed to do?

I feel alright driving. Definitely weak and cautious of sudden movements because I don't want the blood gushing out of me. It's a very short trip. I grab the biggest pads they sell and some adult diapers. I thought they'd be easier because a pad just isn't enough right now. You think they would make something for women that works.

I think back to when Madison said the government would poison us. I'm beginning to believe she was onto something.

The road in front of me looks weird. It's all wonky. It's fine. You're fine. Don't overthink it, Marabelle. My eyes struggle to stay open, but thankfully I make it home. By the time I reach my bedroom, I'm winded. My vision closes in. Before I can get to my bed to crawl into a ball, my body slams the floor, and I faint.

I'm groggy and confused as I wake. The clock tells me I've been out for about ten minutes. My body tells me I have no external injuries. My mind debates whether I fell asleep from exhaustion or if I really fainted. If I fainted, something really is wrong, and maybe I should go to the hospital. That would be 3/4 of the call doctor symptoms. Expect, I can't do that. The hospital will ask what's wrong or what I've taken, and it will go through insurance, and my Mom will know I had an abortion. I think I was really tired. That's one of the common side effects listed on that paper: tiredness. It must have been that. I have to be fine. The hospital is not an option.

My phone dings, and I immediately know who it is.

Jace: well

Me: It's over. I was 8 weeks 3 days. I go back in 2 weeks to make sure it's gone.

He sends me a Star Wars meme, the text on the screen reading: truly wonderful the mind of a child.

Is he fucking for real? What kind of a person would do that? What does that even mean? My patience for him has worn thin. I was waiting for him to text me the day I got it done. He knew the date and the time. I never got a text. And I didn't have the energy to fight for one. I'm not sure what could have been more important. My thumbs slam into the keys, responding with:

Me: So you're done. I'll text you in three weeks, so you know 100%.

Jace: Oh, okay.

Me: Unless you don't want to know.

Jace: I want to.
That kid could have been something.

Me: Jace, please don't.

Jace: I know he would have been a stud

    I can't even believe what I'm reading from him. Why is he genderizing it?

Me: Yeah, he would've

Why am I agreeing?

Jace: damn.

Me: I don't even have words right now.
I'm sorry, I'll go.

Jace: Where you gonna go

Me: No idea

Jace: Well, okay

I wish you would come here, Jace. I wish that you would stop making this harder than it is. I wish you still cared about me. I wish you could understand what I have been going through. I wish you didn't make it a joke. You called it a he.

In my visions, it was a he too.

CHAPTER TWENTY-EIGHT

"Hi, Sweetie." My Mom enters my room. "You okay? Are you not feeling well?" She questions.

My back is turned to her. I'm wrapped in the warmth of my blankets. I really don't want to break free from my comfort, but I have to dismiss this so she doesn't pick up on anything.

I roll over to face her, sitting up slightly in my bed. "Yeah, I think I got the stomach bug. I was feeling so nauseous in school, and by the time I got home, I started to run a fever."

"Shit. Do you think it's going around at school? I can take off of work tomorrow and take you to the doctor-"

Tell her, Marabelle.

No, no, no! Shut up! I can't tell her she would freak. It doesn't matter what kind of relationship you have with your Mom. It's like every mother's worst nightmare to hear that their teenage daughter is pregnant, right? I'm a good girl. I drink a little and smoke a lot, but I get my shit done. I have never betrayed her, and this would have been a betrayal. Good girls don't get pregnant like this. It's too late.

"No, no, Mom, I'm okay. Kids from the play had it last week. They all said it's a 48-hour thing. It'll run its course." I promise.

"That damn play!" She shakes her head. "I guess you guys are in such close quarters and together every day that when one gets it, you all do."

"Yeah," I say.

"Well, I made you some dinner, a little rice. Hopefully, you can hold it down." She places the food tray on my nightstand. "You need anything else, my love?"

I need you to tell me everything is going to be okay and that I'm not having some freak reaction to the abortion pills. That the amount I'm bleeding is normal for murder. I need you to tell me that the pain goes away, Mom. I want you to apologize for being absent all weekend and for not being able to see my suffering. I need you, Mom. I need someone.

"I think I'm okay, thank you."

"Get some rest, baby," she kisses me on the forehead, "text or shout if you need anything."

I want to tell her. I beg for someone to understand the weight of what is happening. Could she be so blind, or could I be a conniving mastermind?

CHAPTER TWENTY-NINE

It's time for this to all be over. Fourteen days have passed since the procedure. My fever stopped seven days ago. I stopped bleeding three days ago.

My absences at play rehearsal have gotten me into a little bit of trouble. I gave no excuse for them. My energy to lie is running out.

Eli has texted me a bunch of times, but I was busy bleeding, shaking, and sobbing. Mrs. Welsh threatened to give the understudy my role if I missed another rehearsal. I didn't know she could be so strict. I don't blame her. I was a no-show when I could've simply told her I was sick. Or something like being sick.

I wound up calling the abortion clinic after Easter to make sure my symptoms were normal. They were very alarmed by what I was describing and encouraged me to come in right away. I didn't want to. I thought I could beat it, but the fear was too strong.

They told me that my body was rejecting the medication, so they gave me some steroids to counteract the symptoms. They emphasized how important it was for me to come back at the two-week mark to ensure everything inside was back to normal. They used the word normal.

The giant cold wand is being reinserted into my vagina one final time.

"Alright, honey, it looks like your uterus is all clear." The doctor smiles.

"So I'm not pregnant anymore?" I'm in shock.

"No, everything looks good. Your body handled the medication well. You are all set to go."

I have no words other than "Okay." I want to get out of here as quickly as I can.

I don't look back. I break free from the doors and let the Spring air fill my lungs. I'm waiting for the freedom to kick in. To feel lighter, and brighter, and more at peace. My mind tries to get there, but I crash into a wall of guilt every single time. I break out into a sprint, racing to get to my car. Each step is full of shame, each stride emphasizing my disgust. What have I done? It's over now; everything looks good. But what about how I feel, doctor? Because I feel like I'll never be the same again. The could've been is haunting me. It dangles its hope right in front of me.

Let me out. Let me out. Let me out.

Please, I can't think about it anymore. I can't feel it.

Jace

I'm excited to spend Spring break on campus. There's too much drama at home, it's better for me to stay here. I talked to some of the frat guys, and they said a lot of people stay on campus; it's like party central. I need some partying. After midterms, I feel worn out and ready for some beer. Today was our last exam and I couldn't have felt better handing it in. I grabbed a spot in the courtyard outside to wrap up some tutoring emails before I plot what's going down tonight. My phone buzzes in my pocket.

Belle: It's done. You're off the hook.

I completely forgot. She went today to make sure it's gone.

Me: Okay

It's done. The feeling of freedom consumes me. I throw my head back in triumph and feel the cool Spring air bless me.

I close my laptop and call Belle. I want to hear her voice.

"Hello?" She sounds confused.

"Hi."

"What do you want, Jace?"

"Jeez, don't get too excited."

"I'm not trying to be a dick right now. I'm really not. You just don't understand."

"Okay.." I trail off.

She explodes, cutting me off before I can get another word in, "Are you not even going to acknowledge what is going on or even try to be there for me? This whole fucking thing has shown me who you really are."

I look around to make sure no one is close enough to hear me. "I don't know what you would like me to do, Belle. Like, I'm not that person. If you don't know that by now, I don't know how to explain it to you. I'm not going to sit here and baby you and be like are you okay? You need shit like that, but I don't," I get loud. "Because I don't want people doing that shit for me. If you need help with something, you text or call me and ask."

"Jace I don't expect you to baby me. I expected you to acknowledge that I was pregnant with your kid and had to have an abortion all by myself with no support when the only person I needed was you. I didn't need a pity party I just needed you to tell me I was going to be okay."

"You were going to be okay. I knew that from the start," I attest.

She's screaming at me, "I needed to hear that from you. Nothing will ever be the same, Jace. I will never be the same."

"I really think you're gassing this whole thing up," I confess. I don't know why she isn't happy, relieved that it's over and done with.

She pauses, waiting for me to say more. She inhales and says defeated, "I don't think you're understanding the situation at all."

"Belle, stop, you're being dramatic. If you wanted to give birth to it, you could have, and I would have taken it, like you could have done either or. You had a choice!"

Marabelle

A choice.

We make choices each and every day: what we should eat for breakfast. How sweet we want our coffee to be. What clothes will protect our bodies best from the weather. Tiny, microscopic decisions that keep us moving. Some days, we have big choices to make, like whether you should quit your job or not. If you should call the police after getting into a fender bender. How much money you need to budget to pay your bills. Choices are constantly flowing through us as human beings, the spectrum of them ranging very wide.

You had a choice.

The choice between life and death.

The choice between an abortion or a baby.

The choice to keep or adopt.

The choice between myself and you.

The choice between losing myself or raising you.

The choice to have an abortion is never something that should be taken away.

You didn't give me a choice. You never asked me what I wanted to do. You never told me that keeping it was an option. And then I get an abortion, and this whole time, you make it all so real for me. Calling it a baby, giving it a gender. You said you would take it? What the fuck makes you think that I would let that happen. If you couldn't be there for it, unborn, what the hell gives you the audacity to say that? Did you think that I couldn't feel how real this was? My body started to change giving me signals and signs to protect and claim, when I knew all along that I was going to abandon and refute. You do not get to say those things to me, Jace. You do not get to downplay my experience. It's not that I wanted to keep it; it's that the choice has left me devastated in its path.

The truth is no one knows what they are getting into when they make the choice for either side of the coin. It's a whirlwind no matter what direction you go. You will be judged and ridiculed no matter which way you turn. It will be hard on your mind, body, and soul either way. The beauty of being a woman is that no man will ever be able to wrap their small brains around what we go through. I hoped that even if he couldn't feel exactly what I felt both mentally and physically, then he could at least empathize with what I am trying to explain.

A jagged sob escapes my lips, "I have to go, Jace. Don't even worry about the money at this point. Goodbye," and I end the call.

I play no music while driving home. I say nothing. I cry for me. I cry for a baby that could have been. I cry for every woman on this planet.

The Finale

CHAPTER THIRTY

"There's something different about you, Belle," Joey circles my face. "I can't put my finger on it," he taps the point of my nose.

"Or maybe," I say, removing his finger from my face, "you're just wasted."

"Well, that's definitely true. But I noticed it before that, haha."

"It's her hair, idiot," Brandon slaps Joey on the back of his head. "She straightened her hair."

I knew it was naive to think no one would notice. I wanted to feel different, so I straightened my hair for tonight's party. My hair has to be straight anyway for opening night this week, so I figured tonight was a good test run.

I had Lindsay do it so that way it would look presentable. I could've done it, but I knew it wouldn't look this good. She was so excited to do it because she knew I never let her touch my curls. I didn't mind hanging out with my little sister for three hours. I've been hanging out with her any chance I get nowadays. She's the only one I can feel at ease around. Her innocence blinds my impurity.

"Belle, let's go grab you a drink. You look like you need one," Elena laces her arm in mine, and we walk into the raging house.

This party is so big I don't even know the person who's throwing it. Apparently, they wanted the entire senior class here. They did not disappoint.

A massive open living room holds the main crowd of people. Beautiful arches all around the home lead into tiny pockets upstairs. It seems like a combination of every social hierarchy at the school combined, which is unusual for Titan. We all usually stick to our own lanes. Since graduation is getting closer and closer, our beliefs about each other are starting to simmer.

"Belle tequila or vodka?"

"Vodka Elena! Come on." I roll my eyes.

"Silly question." She pours our drinks. "I've been meaning to ask you, have you spoken to Jace since—you know, that last phone call?"

I close my eyes, chugging the drink she made for me, and slide the empty cup back to her. "No. And I really don't want to talk about it."

She nods once, questions lingering behind her eyes. I continue, "Any of it." And swallow the second glass she so obediently refilled.

I know what Elena thinks about all of this. She hates Jace, thinks he's a piece of shit. Her feelings are valid, but she decided through this whole process she is not tolerating him anymore. She asks me to tell her stuff about what's going on with him and then dismisses it like she wasn't the one who brought it up. It's frustrating. I can't talk about it anymore. I can't feel it.

Drink after drink, we divulge in the activities that make us teenagers. People branch off to go hookup, couples are fighting every which way you turn, and I just joined a game of never have I ever.

It's a classic: if you have done whatever is said, then you drink and put a finger down. My friend group usually suggests this game at parties because it's a great way to get dirt on people and then discuss it afterward. Brandon, Joey, Elena, Madison, and Kelly have taken up some theater people in conversion. I said hi to Tabitha and Eli, so naturally, I figured it wasn't the worst time for introductions between my two groups. I haven't spoken much. I actually don't even know what they're all giggling about. I zoned out, allowing the rhythmic beats to fill my head and let it bob side-to-side.

"So, are we playing or what?" I shout to the groups.

"Yeah, let's start. Everyone got a drink?" Eli asks. "Okay, I'll go first. Never have I ever smoked weed?"

"What the fuck."

"Is he for real?"

"You have to be lying, Eli."

Eli shrugs with a devilish smirk on his face, "Seriously, I've never smoked weed before, but I know all of you have, so let's see those fingers down and those drinks up."

I drink and put a finger down.

Madison's next to Eli, so we go around the circle. "Ummm-umm. This is hard. Ah-never have I ever...No, wait, I did that." She giggles. "Um—"

"Never have I ever cheated on someone." Joey interrupts Madison. She clearly couldn't spit it out. They glare at each other across the circle, I'm sure they'll kiss about it later.

Tabitha and two other guys drink and drop their fingers. I lean forward to see her full figure, "Damn, Tabitha, I like your savage side." She shrugs her shoulders and playfully rolls her eyes at me.

"Alright, my turn," Elena announces, "Never have I ever gone skinny dipping."

I drink and drop another finger. The burn trickles down my throat, creating a nice coating of manageable pain. I've been keeping myself in a slight state of pain in some way. It helps me leave and come back to my body with no repercussions.

The game goes and goes until we're all in a state of delusion. Some people's feelings are getting hurt, but it's a game. Everyone is way too sensitive. My eyes keep wandering around the house, hoping that Nick might be here. I know this isn't his usual party scene, but it's none of ours. I basically told him to fuck off the last time I saw him, but that doesn't mean I haven't thought about him.

Eli bumps my shoulder, "Drink." I drink.

"What was it?" I ask.

"Never have I ever been in a play."

"Ooooh," I say in a singsong voice. "Well, technically, the play hasn't happened yet, so I didn't need to drink. Depending—de—depending on what they meant," I stutter. "Would then depend on if I drink or not." I conclude.

He laughs at me, "How much have you had to drink, Belle?"

"Shut up," I look up at him and pout my tongue.

"If Eli and Belle would stop flirting, then we could keep the game moving," Brandon says sarcastically to the group.

Eli raises his hand in defense, "Jealousy is not attractive on you my friend. How many people have one finger left?"

We all look around at each other. I have one, Eli has one, and a handful of other people.

Eli continues, "Never have I ever had a pregnancy scare."

It feels like the Earth's axis has broken. We not only stopped spinning, but we've turned on our side and are rolling around space like a bowling ball about to crash into the gutter. What the fuck. Why the fuck did he say that? Madison basically dropped her drink on the ground. Kelly grabbed Elena's arm, and Elena's jaw is on the floor. The common denominator between them is that all their eyes are locked on me.

I don't drink. I don't put my heavy finger down. I pretend like absolutely nothing has changed. Not me, I haven't. I have chills at the word pregnancy. I'm disgusted by the acknowledgment from Kelly and Madison.

Eli did this on purpose. He has to know. Maybe one of them told him. I did see little Miss Big Mouth Madison yapping his ear off early. It's not like I haven't been flaky at rehearsal. I did confide in him about Mrs. Welsh threatening to give my part to the understudy. Eli could have been fishing around for info as to why I've been all over the place. What a fucking snake he is. I can feel my thoughts fueled by the liquor.

I want him to hurt. I want him to feel the amount of embarrassment and shame being spit in my face right now.

No one moves, no one drinks.

"I guess I'm next." My words are laced with malice. "Never have I ever had sex."

The group breaks into laughter—such a ridiculous question for a room full of eighteen-year-olds.

"Really, Belle, I'm sure everyone here has had sex."

"No way anyone's a virgin," Kelly says, laughing.

I look up briefly, trying to find something to bring me back to my humanity. Of course, by the neglect of God, I see Nick descending from the staircase above us. There's a girl with a short brown bob following closely behind him. She's got an athletic little build on her. Maybe that's his new prodigy. Could that be his ex-girlfriend? My brain scans to remember what she looked like from her Instagram, but I can't make the connection. The alcohol won't let me get back there.

I could have stopped there. I could have made Eli feel unintentionally uncomfortable and let him lie to the group. But that's not what I did.

"Go ahead, Eli," I turn to face him, "take a sip and put down your finger."

He turns to me, stunned by my words, confused by my betrayal. I'm confused, too, but the girl screaming to come through and show it has been chained up inside me. My eyes assess him. He's livid. He's backed into a corner. All eyes are on him. He never breaks eye contact with me as he finishes his drink and whips it to the ground before me. The remnants in the cup splash onto my light blue Levi's. Eli disappears into the crowd.

Everyone is looking at me, waiting to see what I will do. I wish people would just react genuinely instead of always following my lead. I manipulate the power they present to me and make sure they understand this is all a big joke. I start cracking up, and my friends follow closely behind me. The theater kids are more hesitant to join in. Some of them can see my calculated move. I don't like that. That means I have a weakness, and no one can know my weaknesses. Tabitha and the girl who plays Peg start to walk away from our group.

Tabitha says, "I think we're going to go grab more drinks, maybe play a different game." Her shoulder brushes mine, and she whispers to me, "Not cool, Marabelle," and she walks off.

The game's momentum is lost, and a million side conversations are happening. No one is taking the initiative to get it going again, so it's whatever. I'm honestly more concerned with finding Nick. Regardless of that brunette tailing him, I need to speak to him.

"Hey guys, I'm going to try and get this red shit off my jeans, be right back." No one follows me.

These are my favorite pair of jeans. I've had these jeans since I started high school. They're the kind of jeans that make you feel good when you put them on. Not too tight on the tummy, enough suction on the ass, and the perfect wash for my skin tone. Today, when I put on these jeans, they didn't fit like they normally do. It was a tight squeeze to get them in place over my hips. I have wide hips; it's my favorite feature, but recently, my stomach and hips have become one.

When I put on these jeans before, it was the first time I became hyper-aware of my body. I know I have a good body, and I've always enjoyed using it to get what I want, but today was different. I didn't love every part of my body. I felt a sting of insecurity nest itself inside of my brain. Normally, I'm a pants and tiny top kind of girl. Tonight, I'm wearing slightly too-tight jeans and a barely cropped shirt.

The red marks from Eli's drink won't come out. The toilet paper is just crumbling in my hands, and there's no soap in this bathroom, so it's fucking useless. Eli's got to be upset with me. I reacted because I felt attacked. I'm upset with him, too. How could he know that I was pregnant? Why wouldn't he ask me himself instead of humiliating me in front of everyone? I think I played it off, though. I hope no one caught on.

Nick looked so sexy. He's always dressed with a bit of skater-boy flair. The first night I met him, he wore those same beat-up jeans. I wonder if he distresses them himself. That would make him even hotter. There's not much that wouldn't make Nick hot. He is the epitome of man. I have to know if I fucked that up for good. I need to find him, and I definitely need to get rid of that brunette.

Stumbling out of the bathroom door, the heat of the party encases my flesh. I shimmer through the crowd of people going in the opposite direction of my friends. I grab a drink along the way and down it. I shouldn't drink anymore, but my hands keep grabbing them, and my throat keeps swallowing, so I've lost control.

I can't find Nick. I've casually searched this whole house, and I have no idea where he went. There's a possibility he left. He doesn't seem like one to stay for a while at parties. That's according to the track record he's shown me. Well, to be fair, that last one's on me, but—

"What the fuck was that Belle?" Eli grabs my arm and pulls me into the hallway.

"Jesus Eli," I throw his hand off of me, "I told you to never touch me like that again."

"Yeah, well, I'm pissed, so I really don't care what you told me. What I told you was a secret. How could you exploit one of my secrets like that? I trusted you."

"I-I- you were," I take a deep breath. "Can we go outside, please? Let's not do this in here," I say, tilting my head towards the girls staring at us.

We walk out the back door. There's a couple of people outside, but not enough to pay any attention to us.

"So what bullshit excuse are you going to give me, Belle, huh? Little Miss Perfect didn't get everything she wanted tonight, so she had to pick on someone to feel good about herself again?" Eli's tone is a mockery.

"I'm not the one who went digging for dirt on someone I considered to be a friend," I motion between the two of us. "Who told you? Was it Madison? If you tell me it was Elena Eli, I am going to fuck her up."

"What are you even talking about, Belle? You're fucking wasted speaking nonsense. This is about you telling everyone in there I'm a virgin. It was fucking humiliating. I thought we were friends. I thought we genuinely had become really close friends. I thought you dropped this whole mean girl act—"

"Mean girl act? This isn't some character development bullshit. I'm the same girl I was when you met me at auditions. I'm the same girl who you tried to flirt with and got denied. I'm the same girl you confided in and trusted. I didn't change. Nothing about me has changed!"

He steps into me very, very slowly. He opens his mouth, but it takes a second for words to come out. "Then why are you crying, Belle?"

I squint in confusion. I raise my hand and suddenly feel the wetness as it drips from my eyes.

My body has betrayed me. Funneling out what I am trying so hard to keep in.

I thought we had a mutual agreement to shut it off. If you need to come up, come up in anger, not tears.

Using the support of the house, I sink to the floor. "Who told you I was pregnant?"

He squats down in front of me, barricading me in. "You're pregnant?"

"Was."

CHAPTER THIRTY-ONE

The tears pour out of my eyes, and I try to catch my breath. My breath hitches with each inhale, unable to get oxygen inside my body. It's the kind of cry that scares people. The cry that can't be stopped but can be felt around the world.

I try to make out the sounds around me. Muffled words break through my thoughts, but I don't know who's saying them or where they're coming from. I'm spiraling in a black hole of terror.

"Breathe, Belle," I hear a tiny voice trying to soothe me and a hand on my back applying tight compression.

I lost control. The floodgates have opened.

I really think you're gassing this whole thing up.

It was a clump of cells. It wasn't a baby. I didn't do anything wrong. Why do I feel like I did something wrong? Am I gassing this whole thing up?

You're being dramatic.

Maybe I am being dramatic. Maybe my pain and suffering have been exaggerated in my mind. Maybe I took on the role of the victim too hard. Am I making this a bigger deal than it is? Is Jace right?

"Belle!"

I know how I felt before. I know how I felt during. To feel like this after isn't dramatic. They want you to think it isn't a big deal. A quick and easy procedure. In and out, no fuss. You'll be back to "normal" after. Nothing about this is normal, and no one wants you to talk about it.

"Belle, breathe, we're almost home." Eli hasn't taken his hand off of me.

My crying has exhausted me into silent tears. They fall every once in a while, requiring no effort on my part.

"Here, drink this," Eli hands me a glass of water, "do you want a blanket or anything?"

"I'm sorry," I manage to say.

"Belle, please don't apologize, I-." He hands me one of his hoodies. "I don't want to push, but you told me you were pregnant and then started having a panic attack. I got you out of there as soon as I could. You were making no sense in the car screaming through cries about Jace? And being dramatic?"

I had no idea I was talking out loud. I can barely piece together anything after seeing Nick.

We're on the floor in Eli's room, sitting on a black carpet. It's tiny in here, only room for a twin bed and some awards on a shelf. Eli's body is too big for a twin bed.

"You drove here?" I ask.

"Yeah."

"But we're drunk. You shouldn't have driven."

"I didn't know what to do, Belle. You were hyperventilating. My Mom used to have horrible panic attacks, and I know that it's best not to have a crowd around in the middle of one. I figured you didn't want the whole party to see." He takes a sip of water. "Is that what that was? A panic attack?"

I throw his hoodie on over my clothes. I feel too exposed. It's warm, and it smells like fresh laundry. "I'm not sure. I kind of blacked out," I shrug. "I've never had one of those before."

Panic attack, I didn't know they were called that.

"I'm sorry I told everyone you're a virgin. I thought you knew I was pregnant and said that to hurt me."

"I would never do that, Belle, even if I did know."

"I think I'm losing my mind, Eli."

"What happened?" He asks, sincerity laced in his tone.

I exhale loudly and place the glass of water down next to me. I explained the night I found out I was pregnant. Eli listens. Occasionally nodding along, but for the most part, listens.

"When I told Jace, he didn't believe it was his. Honestly, he brought that up a lot. I get it. I know how people can perceive me."

"Yeah, but if he really knows you, Belle, he wouldn't have even questioned it."

"And that's the part that hurts the most. So I went to get an abortion, and they told me I was too early, so I had to wait. I waited 4 weeks because that was the earliest appointment time I could find."

"So you were pregnant that whole time? Every rehearsal, every ride to school, every— everything. That's a huge weight to carry."

"Yes," I nod. "Jace would text me and say fucked up things like it's a baby boy, or send me inappropriate memes about how much of a "stud," I quote Jace, the baby would've been."

"What the fuck." Eli looks disgusted.

"Yeah, so then I finally had the abortion, and it was incredibly painful; I got pretty sick, and—" I trail off, severing the memory of pain. "I did it alone. It was the week I skipped rehearsal, and Mrs. Welsh threatened to replace me. There were so many moments when all I wanted was a *are you okay* from him. Nothing big, but something. You know?"

"Of course, I know. I don't think you're being dramatic about this at all, Belle. I actually think you're being quite subtle. This guy, Jace, is a total asshole. You were pregnant and had to have an abortion because who the fuck is having a kid at eighteen? You did what you had to do for you," he pauses, "and for fucking him. He can't even give you the decency of support? Nah, that's absolutely fucked. At the very least, he could've asked if you needed anything. Did he come and see you at all?"

"Not once. He didn't even pay for it. Said he would, but—" I throw my hands up.

"I'm so sorry, Belle. I wish you would've told me sooner. I would have been there for you."

"Well, I never planned to tell anyone at all. Only Jace, Madison, Kelly, and Elena know. If I wasn't such a bitch, I would've never blurted it out to you. I lost control."

This is something I swore I would take to the grave.

A tear drops. He scooches over and brings me into a hug. I lean into him, allowing some release through our embrace. "Thank you, I don't deserve this."

"You do. You deserve so much more than what he gave you," he whispers.

We stay like that for a while. I feel validated like every feeling I've felt is reasonable.

Sometimes, I do feel like I can be too much. Jace always made me feel like I was too much. Like I give too much love, like I'll never be enough. It's nice to have the perspective of an outsider.

"You can sleep here if you don't want to be alone. I'll sleep on the floor. You can take the bed."

"I'll sleep on the floor, and you sleep in your bed, Eli," I let out a small smile.

"Alright, I was trying to be a gentleman."

"It's shocking for me, considering I'm only used to assholes."

We laugh, and the heaviness of the room lifts slightly. My body feels heavy on the ground, relaxing quickly like it was waiting for this moment. My eyes droop, and sleep comes to get me. Right before I drift away, Eli whispers, "Hey, Belle."

"Mmm."

He murmurs, "Everything is going to be okay."

CHAPTER THIRTY-TWO
Jace

My body gets flung to the opposite side of my car. The impact leaving me confused and startled. It takes me a second or two to process what happened. Someone's black truck is smashed into the front of my Mustang. My car is on a slight angle upwards, fighting gravity not completely to tip over. I look to my left and see a guy getting out of his truck. My door is smashed, so I climb over my center console and get out on the passenger side.

"What the fuck, man?" This old guy says.

"Bro you were flying. You smashed right into me." I'm fucking pissed. This old fuck just destroyed my car.

The rational side of my brain isn't a fool. I know that, technically, this accident is my fault. I was inching out to cross the intersection. I was probably sticking out too far. Under the law, it's my fault, but according to me, it's his. I take a long blink, remembering that I drank tonight and how much. If I lose my temper with this guy, he's definitely calling the cops.

I turn on my charm. "My bad, bro. Obviously, looking at my car does not feel good right now," I point at the mess in front of us. "It's a tough intersection," I say, shrugging.

"I know, man, no one wants to end their night like this. I'm Tom," he reaches his hand out to shake mine. "I can give you my information if you want to handle things off the books before the cops show up."

"I'm cool with that. Whatever the estimate is," I nod. "I'll take care of it. Let me know." I take down his name and number and he takes a photo of my license and our cars.

He shakes my hand again, "Between me and you, I'm doing you a favor. I can smell the liquor on you, boy. I'll get the statement for my car and accept the money from you in cash. If you don't pay up, I will get the police involved."

I nod my head in understanding. "I'll get you the money."

A series of unfortunate events can sum up this year. I had the money for Belle. It's wrapped in a rubber band sitting in my sock drawer. I worked way too many hours at the student center to get her that money. I haven't been home in months because of it. I told her I was getting her the money, so I will give her that money.

I planned to give it to her this weekend. I'm supposed to leave tomorrow morning to head back home for a couple of nights. What the frat guys failed to mention about Spring break on campus is that, eventually, everyone gets burnt out. We've been partying for the last five days. The weather was gorgeous, and the girls were looking great. Now that the forecast says rain the rest of the week, everyone is going home.

It's 2 am when I make it back to the dorms. My drive back was sketchy. I was nervous my busted car was going to crap out. I was even more nervous a cop would see my demented car, pull me over, and breathalyze me. I checked every mirror a hundred times.

I go to open my door, but something stops it. "Yo, Jace! I thought you weren't coming back tonight." Oliver shouts from inside our room.

"Yeah, man, plans changed." I apply force to the door, but it doesn't budge. "What the fuck is this? Open the door."

"Sorry, man, I got someone in here. I texted you before."

I don't even hear him attempting to get up. "Oliver, I'm not in the fucking mood. Move the goddamn dresser before I break this door down!" I start pounding on the door. Loud enough to scare whatever girl he has inside of there. Loud enough to wake up our whole floor.

"Yo Jace, man fucking relax. Give us a second to get dressed," Oliver shouts.

"I don't have a fucking second. You open this door right fucking now!" My fists bang on the door. "Why the fuck is there a barricade up? You ashamed of the ugly bitch you got in there?"

"Excuse me, do we have a problem here?" Our dorm advisor comes to stand beside me.

I look her up and down. She's cute. Big curly brown hair, glasses, and sweatpants on. Her red, watery eyes tell me I must've woken her up. She kind of reminds me of Belle if I squint a little. I wonder what Belle is doing right now.

"No problems," I say, throwing my hands up in defense. She looks scared. "I hope I didn't cause any trouble. Don't worry, I'm leaving."

Walking away, I hear Oliver through the door, "Don't write him up, Alice, he's been going through some stuff. Just let him go."

I seek shelter in my car. My poor baby, my absolute pride and joy. This Mustang was my Grandpa's. It had been promised to me before I could even walk. Getting this car when I turned seventeen changed everything for me. I had freedom. I could pick up girls and drive them around. I can't count how many of them I hooked up with in this very back seat. High school hookups in a car are a cannon event. My cannon event was on repeat.

I recline my seat all the way back and light the joint I rolled. Closing my eyes softly, I inhale. My left shoulder throbs. It took the brunt of the impact, so I'm sure that's why I can feel my blood pulsing there. I didn't notice I was in so much pain until this joint let me feel it. How the fuck am I going to pay for that guy's car? How the fuck am I going to pay for both of our cars? I'm so fucked.

I text Belle.

Me: Hey

She's the only person I need right now, the only one who could help. She always knows what to do and always has a solution for me. I've never felt so taken care of by someone in my life. She does everything I ask and then some. It's one of the things I love most about her.

I do love her. I was a little annoyed with her for her theatrics, but that doesn't mean she still isn't mine. I haven't really been able to process what happened. I pushed it into a dark corner inside me. All I know is that it's over, and I'll never have to think about it again, at least until I get her this money. It's going to have to wait. It's not like she needs the money in order to get the abortion. She already got the abortion; it's already taken care of; it's a matter of me paying my debt.

It's the right thing to do. I told her I would pay for it, so I will pay for it. I'm going to have to take up an extra job or two. It's going to be bread to fix that guy's car. I shouldn't have left that party drunk. I could've slept there. I was starting to think about Belle, and whenever I think about her in public, I start freaking out like I lost my game, and I can't talk to any girls.

"Wakey wakey, drunkie," Oliver taps on my passenger window.

I slowly make my way out of the car.

"You look horrible, what the fuck happened here?"

The thing about boys is that we don't need a whole song and dance about our little run-in last night. There's nothing to talk about, nothing to discuss. He clearly doesn't care, so I don't either.

"I got into an accident," I roll my eyes. Oliver has a big duffle bag slung over his shoulder. If I play this right, he'll drop me off at home on his way through Jersey.

"You're heading home?" I ask.

"Yeah."

"Can I get a ride since you gotta pass through Jersey anyway?"

"Sure, but I'm only staying for a couple of days," Oliver says.

"That's all I need. Just scoop me on your way back?"

"I can do that, come on."

CHAPTER THIRTY-THREE
Marabelle

We're all seated in a semi-circle around Mrs. Welsh. She has extra enthusiasm and sass today as we're days out from the opening night. I'm feeling confident in my role. Playing Tess Coleman has been the easier part of my year. It's a form of escapism that allows me to feel the emotions of someone other than myself.

Eli's to my left, propped up against the stage setup. He always gets yelled at for doing that. A barrier has broken between the two of us after the other night. It's not romantic by any means. It feels like my first genuine friendship. He sees all of me and accepts it. Even after I hit him in his most vulnerable spot, that was not my best moment. I'll continue to apologize for it.

"Ladies and gentlemen, I am beyond proud of the work we have created so far. Tabitha and Belle, you two were meant to be on stage together like Anna and Tess. Thank you for making my vision come to life."

Everyone breaks out in applause. Mrs. Welsh continues, "So tomorrow, eighth period, you will all be pulled out of class for our dress rehearsal. We will do one walk-through Friday afternoon, and then you'll go home and be back here by 6 pm sharp. The costume and stage crew will need to arrive at 5:45 for setup. All the details have been put in the group chat, so if your teenage minds forget what I have continuously gone over, check there."

I giggle to myself. Mrs. Welsh is unique. She has a beautiful way of treating us like adults but reminding us we're kids at heart. She makes everything lighter.

"And that's all I have for you," she claps her hands together. "You're free to go. I'll see your souls tomorrow eighth period."

Eli and I haven't given up on carpooling. He drives most days because he claims I'm always running late. "Did you ever text Jace back from the other night?"

"No. It was the middle of the night. I didn't see it until we woke up that morning. He was probably drunk, so it couldn't have been good."

"He was definitely drunk. He texted you at like 3 am."

It's been nice to confide in Eli completely candidly. The weight of the secret has lifted by one pound. I can't talk like this with Elena. She doesn't understand.

"If I was awake, I would've answered," I confess.

"Why?" He asks with no judgment present.

"Cause, I don't know. I still care about him," I rub my fingers over my temples, "I know I'm not supposed to. I know what he did was fucked up, but I feel like I need closure. Maybe a damn apology."

"You do need closure, based on what you told me. How things ended with him was not good. Or if they even ended at all. He still feels like he can text you. Maybe you need to end it for good. "

"Yeah, it was weird. I honestly don't know if there is a for good with us." I pause and ponder that to myself. I reach no verdict. I continue, "It's hard for me to remember what I love about him."

Eli gives me a sideways look, "I can't think of one goddamn thing!"

We both burst into laughter.

"His dick games got to be strong," he teases.

"It was," I scream up into the air. "Maybe I do remember one thing."

"Alright, get out of my car, Belle, and spare me the details," Eli unlocks the door.

"Thank you, I'll see you tomorrow."

"Later."

No one's ever home after school. I take advantage of that, grabbing my stash from my room and rolling a quick joint for myself. The weather is getting nicer every day. Smoking outside in this weather is healing. I puff the joint down, taking intermissions to sip out of a Capri Sun. By the time the joint is done, I have officially escaped.

I like being up here better. I always liked it, but lately, the disconnect from mind to body brings me so much peace. It allows me to feel less and smile more. Sometimes, when I'm up here, my thoughts can spiral me back down. The tornado comes to grab me and ropes me back in, stronger and more ruthless than before.

I should've texted Jace back. Something could've happened to him. I wonder if it's too late to text him. Did he text because he finally has the money for me? Maybe he misses me and wanted to hear my voice. I haven't seen him in so long. We've only gone one other time without seeing each other for this long. I want to talk to him. I need him to understand exactly what happened to me. If he knows the details, maybe he'll understand why I feel the way I do. He's contacted me more since it's been over than during. He doesn't deserve my attention, but he has it. He'll always have it.

Hours passed. I ate dinner with my family. My Dad was actually there. He told me he's coming to watch the play Friday night. I think he expected some grand reaction, like he's doing me a favor by being there. I was cold to him, as I usually am.

It's hard for me to look into my Father's eyes recently. He's the only man in our house, and he's barely even there. To be a man in this world is a privilege. He has that privilege over all of us. My Mom always makes comments about how he's a "good Father," but she can't possibly believe that. I guess it depends on what she classifies as good. She runs this entire family, does everything for us. Does the woman always have to do everything? Do we have to carry the weight of the world on our backs and look pretty while we're doing it?

I am envious that Jace doesn't have to feel an ounce of repercussions. Not before. Not during. Not after. I wonder if he thinks about it if it ever crosses his mind. I'm curious if when he thinks about me, I'm immediately associated with that. He has to think about me, even if it's a fraction of how much I think about him.

There's not a day that goes by that I don't think about the abortion.

I keep waiting for the day to wake up and not feel the hole growing inside me. That day hasn't come yet. I'm beginning to lose hope of that day.

"I love your hair straight, Marabelle. I don't know why you don't wear it like this more often." My Mom sits on my bedroom floor, leaning against the foot of my bed.

"I love my curls, Mom, you know that," I assure.

"I know. I mean, look who you got them from," she fluffs up her hair. "It's just different, a good change-up for big events."

Lindsay chimes in, "The play is a big event. I'm so excited for Friday. I invited all of my dance friends, Belles. I hope you don't mind."

"Oh god," I laugh. "Twelve-year-olds are the toughest critics of all. I'm going to have to be on point."

"I am a pretty tough critic," Lindsay takes down the last section of my hair to re-straighten. She insisted on going over a couple of pieces before tomorrow.

"Who are you playing again?" Mom asks.

"Tess Coleman, Jaime Lee Curtis played her in the actual movie."

"Oh, that's right. Yes, she was great. So why do they want your hair straight if her hair is super short in the movie."

"Well, they said I could wear a wig or straighten it. Mrs. Welsh isn't too big on looking like the part. She thinks our acting should speak for itself."

"Hmm," my Mom nods, "a wise woman."

"Are you going to let me straighten it for graduation? We could do a cute updo with it?"

"I don't know yet, Linds. Graduation is pretty far away," I say.

"No, it's not, sweetie, less than two months. Oh, that reminds me. Aunt Lisa called today. She said your cousin Isabella is planning something at the end of June and wanted to make sure it won't conflict with your graduation party."

"What's Isabella planning?" I ask.

"I'm not sure. She was very cryptic about the whole thing. I told her we didn't plan anything yet for you. So she doesn't have to worry." She trails off. "I think she's pregnant."

Don't panic. Do not react.

"Oh yeah, why do you say that," I ask casually.

"I had a dream the other night that I was playing with a little baby boy. He was adorable, and the whole family was there. We haven't had a baby in the family in so long. Everyone was so happy."

"Awe, I hope she's pregnant. That would be so cute!" Lindsay squeals. "Would that make me an aunt?" She asks.

"Yeah, it has to be a sign or something. Between my dream, Aunt Lisa calling, and the fact that the last time I saw Isabella, she wasn't drinking, I think she's pregnant." Mom is convinced she's nailed it.

Your suspicions could be correct, Mother. Or they could be so very wrong. If the nail is right in front of her, she keeps missing. Banging, and banging, and banging one centimeter off from the head.

How could you be so dumb?

I choke out the words, with a bullet lodged in my throat, a fire burning in my chest, "It would be really nice to have a baby in the family."

They say all these moments happen in life that determine who you are. I've been more affected by them than ever. People's word cut, and they don't even realize it. I don't blame them. How are they supposed to know that I just had an abortion and am highly sensitive right now? My Mom's words hurt. I want her to know, but I would also rather hang myself than have her know. It's too late now. There's nothing she can do for me, nothing she can say to make me feel differently. I've always been able to choke down the genuine side of myself. To let it subside so that my harder exterior could show through. I'm having to reinvent a whole different side of myself. She's darker, scarier. She has way more grit and determination. She can blow at any minute. I need to work on my fuse. I can't be spilling out like I did with Eli. I have to get a better grip on my emotions. Things that help that:

-smoking
-thinking about Nick
-resenting Jace
-hanging out with Eli

I still haven't seen Nick. I haven't been back to open gym in a while. I could only bring myself to do the things I had already committed to. If Mrs. Welsh wasn't so involved with the students, I would've quit as soon as I found out I was pregnant. I didn't have anyone forcing me to go practice at the gym. It was my own personal responsibility. Because I was dealing with the biggest responsibility of my life, I had no room for anything else. There were times that I could hear Nick in my head telling me to funnel my aggression into something good. My anger has turned into sadness. My guilt has turned into sadness. My relief has turned into sadness. Everything is sadness. I am an empty shell coated, drenched, and dipped in sadness.

It's only 6:30. Open gym starts at 7. Yeah, my hair is freshly straightened and needs to look good for the next 3 days, but I want to see Nick. At the very least to apologize for my sudden change of heart.

I'm going, I have to go.

CHAPTER THIRTY-FOUR

The dingy black door welcomes me home. There have been some new additions to the sticker wall that first greeted me when I came here with Nick. Same font reading *MMA Studio 1*, but the red fist has been replaced by an all-black one. Maybe they're under a rebrand. I guess we are all going through a rebrand period.

The gym is packed tonight. Every ring is filled. Nick's not in one of them. I've checked and double-checked four times. We keep missing each other. Our alignment is refusing to connect, and I can't help but feel like it's my fault. I guess I can make the most of it while I'm here.

Punch, block, repeat. That's the only drill we're doing tonight. The people I was practicing with at the last open gym have advanced so much since the last time I was here. They finally moved on to sparring matches. Since my instructor told me I was not ready for that yet, he moved me over to join a different group to learn how to take a hit.

As I'm walking over to them the instructor's face becomes more familiar to me. I feel like I know this guy, but can't quite remember where I know him from. I could have seen him at the gym before. Mostly, everyone is a frequent member. He's staring back at me like he can feel the mutual sense of familiarity.

"Belle," he says to me as he bows his head in greeting. He's not much taller than me, but his energy is powerful. Each muscle under his tank has been formed with time and dedication. His chocolate skin somehow glows under the fluorescent lighting.

"Yeah, that's me," I smile. "Do I know you from somewhere?"

"I'm one of Nick Ricci's good friends," he places his hand on his chest, "my name's Will."

I have seen this boy before. I saw him hop the fence the night of the impostor party and eavesdrop on Nick and I's conversation at Madison's party. Weirdly, times seem simpler then.

"Will, nice to officially meet you. So I got moved to this group because I'm not ready to spar yet."

"Yes, we're practicing brace for impact. Why don't you come join the rest of us? I was about to introduce a breathing exercise."

"Okay, cool." I feel more anxious now than I was when I walked in. In a way, I think Will might be assessing me like he's watching me and taking notes so he can report back to Nick. That could be very conceited of me. I'm sure Nick forgot about me and hasn't thought about me since we last spoke. I did see him with that brunette. I'm sure he's treating her like a fucking princess.

Will starts explaining the importance of breath when fighting. "Being calm and relaxed is the most important thing when it comes to any combat sport. It is therapeutic to be able to let your emotions flow when training MMA, but the best MMA fighters learn to keep their emotions at bay and fight intuitively."

Nothing about me is intuitive. I'm not even sure my intuition functions.

I may have forgotten to mention that this altered side of myself is very pessimistic.

Will continues, "Not panicking when you get hit is key. Being able to funnel the psychical pain you are feeling and replicate it to your opponent is how you'll win."

People nod all around me. This must be resonating for them.

"Alright, we're going to try something. Everyone lay on your backs and close your eyes."

We do as follows. My eyes are the most resistant to shut, but my options are to awkwardly stare at Will or comply.

"It's very loud in here. A lot is going on around us. Inhale and bring your attention inwards. Find that spot inside yourself that brought you here tonight." He pauses. "Now exhale. Keep taking though long inhales and gentle exhales, really dropping into yourself."

I inhale, I exhale, nothing. I follow the smoothness of Will's voice. Will's very attractive. I can't think like that, though. That's Nick's friend. I would get myself into a lot of trouble to even attempt to penetrate their friendship. I've been craving chaos. I want to cause trouble. I want to hurt people. I want someone to feel how I feel.

Inhale and exhale.

I came here tonight to see Nick. My intentions weren't for myself. They were for a boy. To see if that boy still likes me and still wants me. Would I still want me after what I did to him? My thoughts are scattered like broken glass across the floor. I hear punches from the mat next to us. I smell sweaty feet. I think about if my stomach looks fat in the position I'm in. Did Nick get here yet? Did Will tell him that I'm here in the short time I've closed my eyes? I don't trust Will.

"Very good, everyone. Now you should be starting to calm the mind, clearing all thoughts."

Clearing all thoughts? This is stupid. Breathing will not help me clear my thoughts. This is some woo-woo bullshit that doesn't work for people who are actually suffering. I shift my thoughts to Nick's hands on me. While everyone else calms down in their minds, I'll go to a place in mine that brings me slight composure.

It felt so good to have him instruct me with such confidence. I've never been that aroused with a guy before. If he knew we hooked up while

I was pregnant, then he would really never want to talk to me again. How fucked up am I for that? I'm fucked up. I wish my mind would shut the fuck up.

We finish class wiping down the mats. Everyone files out at their own pace. I catch up with Will before it's too late.

"Hey, Will."

"What's up, Belle."

"Um, do you know where Nick has been? I haven't seen him around in a while, and I have been meaning to talk to him."

He nods his head a couple of times and smirks. "I was waiting for that."

"Is it that obvious?"

"I mean," he drags the word, "yeah, it's pretty obvious."

"Awesome," I say sarcastically.

"But yeah, he's been around Belle. I think he's been wondering where you've been. You haven't come to open gym in a while."

"Yeah, I know, I've been really busy."

"I'm sure you have," his tone laced with a little agitation. "You should try texting him. I'm sure he would love to hear from you."

"Really? I don't know." I drop my gaze. "I think I fucked things between us."

Will pushes open the back door, holding it for both of us, "He's a really understanding guy."

"Well, that's true, he's so amazing," I blurt out.

"I'm glad you think so." Ee separate, walking to our cars. Will shouts through the distance, "Between me and you, I'm team Belle and Nick!"

I laugh loud enough for him to hear me. I should reach out to Nick. I guess I didn't end things so badly. He had to have known what he was getting into with me. He said it himself the first night we met. God, that night was magical. I wish I could go back to that night and be that girl again.

I forgot I have no snacks for tomorrow's dress rehearsal. Since I'll be at school all day, I need something to get me through. I could ask Eli to stop tomorrow morning, but I'm sure he'll complain that it'll make us late for the first period.

I pull into the next 24-hour drugstore I see. There's one every 2,000 feet in New Jersey. I step past the all the aisle's. I know I don't need anything else. I B-line right for the gold.

Rounding the corner of the candy section, I freeze. There's the back of Jace's head.

CHAPTER THIRTY-FIVE

My heart is in my throat, or my throat is in my heart. I actually have no idea what is going on inside my body. It feels like all of my insides are battling against each other. I think I might be sick.

He's in a black hoodie, but the hood isn't all the way up. It's puffed up just enough to conceal his full identity. The messy waves of blonde fall perfectly on top of his head. He's approaching the line to check out.

I rip my eyes off of him.

Get your candy, and get out! If he doesn't turn around, he won't ever see you.

I force my eyes to focus on the colorful bags in front of me. The sour gushers are always in the same spot: between the sour patch extremes and the sweet tarts. Looking at the lineup in front of me, they're missing. I sift through to see if maybe they fell behind or underneath or something. The ruffling of the bags is drawing attention to me, slowly increasing my anxiety.

They're not here.

Gusher's are the most classic candy. I grew up eating gushers every day for lunch. Back then, they would come in these tiny little yellow bags containing only about five or six. I remember I used to bite the tip off and squeeze the goo onto my fingers, pretending the goo was my blood.

It wasn't until Jace that I became addicted to the sour ones. They're Jace's favorite. He's obsessed with them. It was always our favorite snack to grab after smoking. He would get them every time we went, so I always dipped into his bag instead of getting my own. He was always quick to share with me. I think it progressed our relationship in a weird, lackluster way. Eventually, Jace learned to get two bags—one for him and one for me.

Did he take all the sour gushers? Is that why there's none here?

I grab whatever is in front of me and go to stand in line. He's about to check out; the only thing separating us is one human soul. My head wants to look down in shame, but my heart longs to see his face. My eyes stay locked on the back of his head as he waits for his items to be rung up.

His Mustang wasn't in the parking lot. At least, I didn't notice it. I would've noticed that beautiful blue car that I know all too well. I shift, scanning the parking lot again, but there's no sign of it. Jace grabs his items, taps his card, and heads for the door.His back presses into it, holding it open for the man who enters next.

I know you can feel me here, Jace.

His motion is guided by his act of kindness. Jace's eyes follow inside, and he nods his head in response to the man's thank you. Picking his head up and ever so slightly turning to the right, we lock eyes. Our alignment connects.

Emotion coats the back of my throat. He stays staring at me as he lets the door close in front of him, separating us by two human souls and a glass door now.

Look away, Belle, look away, pay for this shit so you can get the fuck out of here. I don't know if he's still looking at me. I don't know if he's as flustered as I am. Why is he home? Why is he here? He looked so sad. His eyes were full of shock and remorse. It was like he saw a ghost.

It was like I saw my lover.

We did not see the same things. I did not feel the same way.

I'm supposed to hate him. I'm supposed to want nothing to do with him. Yet all I can bring myself to do is walk out of there as fast as I can before he's gone.

Jace

Shit. I shouldn't have froze like that. I should've fucking run to her. I sit inside my Mom's new car in disbelief at what just happened. She looked so fucking beautiful. Something about her was different. Her hair was straight, which is very unusual for Belle, and she was wearing workout clothes. Has she started going to the gym? That is also very unlike her.

I have a clear shot of her from where my car is positioned. She's paying. Handed the cashier a twenty. I wonder what she was there for because I have the last two bags of sour gushers sitting in my passenger seat. I don't even eat both bags, but it feels wrong only to get one. It was always two, one for me and one for her.

I should go wait for her at her car. I miss her. I want to talk to her. Grabbing the handle, I hesitate. She didn't look like she wanted to talk to me or wanted any part of me for that matter. The last time we spoke, she was screaming at me, and I really don't want that again.

Fuck Belle, how did we get here?

She walking out of the store. I turn the car on and shift it into reverse. I whip out of the spot, crossing the middle of the lot. As she pulls out of her spot, the only thing either one of us can focus on is the other. My car keeps moving, but I keep staring. Very slowly, then all at once, I'm snapped back into reality. I slam on the brake, jolting my head forward. She's studying me, confused by my sudden stop. I whip the car next to hers. I'm not leaving here without talking to her.

I roll down the window, praying that she'll follow my lead. I smile when she does. "Want to get in?" I motion my head towards the passenger seat. A teeny, tiny little smile forms on her delicate face. She rolls her window up and comes to me.

She climbs in, shutting the door and pulling the gushers out from under her butt. "So it was you? You took all the sour gushers and left me with airhead extremes?" She says, holding the bag up.

"Is that what you went there for?"

"Yeah, I needed a snack for school tomorrow."

"That's what I went for too. Well, not school, but a munch for tonight."

"This is a pretty big munch, a Dr. Pepper, and two bags of sour gushers?" Her voice goes up. "Why two?" She drops her tone.

I grab both bags from her hand. I make slight contact with her skin, longing for more of her touch. It sends a bolt of electricity to my dick. "One for me and one for you," I say, offering the other bag to her.

I raise my white flag.

She grabs the bag, immediately opens it, and pops one into her mouth. "Mmm," she moans, "I forgot how good they are."

Belle knows exactly what she does to me. Tonight, she has turned it on to the max, and I'm ready to break.

"So, were you just going to pretend like you didn't see me?" I ask.

"No, obviously I saw you."

"If I didn't let that guy in, you wouldn't have said anything," I say definitively.

"Yeah, I probably wouldn't have. I saw the back of your bean coming from the candy aisle and immediately knew it was you. And then when you opened the door for him, you gave me that look." She says with a flirty grin.

She's not as mad at me as I thought she was.

"Everything's in the eyes, Belle."

She turns her whole body to face me, looking me dead in the eyes, "I know that, Jace. You always say that."

I bring my hand up, gently placing it on the side of her face. I stroke my thumb over her cheeks in a familiar motion. She closes her eyes, the eye contact becoming too intense for me.

"You know what this will lead to," I whisper.

"I know this all too well. I'll stop."

My forehead rests on hers as I respond, "I wish you wouldn't."

"I wish I didn't have to."

"So don't," I confess.

She changes in an instant. Breaking free from my hold and sitting upright. A metal rod shot directly through her spine.

"There's a lot of gray area, Jace. This hasn't been easy for me." She declares.

I don't understand, one minute she was flirty and giggly and embraced my touch. Now she's rigid and angry and can barely look at me.

She continues, "Why are you even home? Where have you been for the last 2 months?"

"I'm home for Spring break."

"Then where's your car? Who's car even is this?"

"Jesus, Belle, I didn't know this was a fucking interrogation."

She ignores my comment and continues to question. "Did you buy this? Did you buy a new car? You're fucking unbelievable. You bought a new goddamn car knowing that you still owe me money. Where the fuck is my money, Jace!"

"Do not raise your voice at me right now. I didn't buy a new car. This is my Mom's new car. I got into an accident. I want you to know that I have to pay seven thousand dollars to fix my car and another thirty-five hundred to fix the other guys. Those are way more important than this," I motion between the two of us. "When I have the money to pay you, I will. Fixing this dude's car isn't on my time, so I can't just be like, yeah I'll give it to you when I get it. I can do that with you. I'm not trying to be a dick Belle. You just don't understand."

"I know nothing about you anymore. I didn't even know you got into an accident. And you are being a dick, Jace. You never checked on me." I can feel the sob about to escape her lips. She's choking it down, trying to keep her emotions at bay. I hate it when she cries.

She shakes her head, letting her anger override her sadness, "YOU don't understand. You have no fucking idea what it was like."

"If I had 600 dollars to just hand you, I would, but you see, in order to hand you money, I have to make the money that can pay for everything. I have to pay for all of it and even more to pay for you. I don't just get handed shit." The bitter words feel wrong to admit to her.

She exhales, annoyed, "I understand you have a lot on your plate, and if you can't pay for it, then just say that." She pauses. "To not even acknowledge the abortion or have been there for me is what hurts. It's not even about the fucking money."

"I will get you the money. That kid was my family, so I have to give you the money."

I'm getting pissed now. She's all over the fucking place. First, it's about the money. Then it's about the abortion. It's like she can't make up her damn mind. I wanted to tell her so bad tonight how much I missed her. I wanted to kiss her and take her back home so we could be together because all of this baby shit is over now. I thought we could go back to the way things used to be. We can't. Nothing is the same. She isn't the same.

"You used to love me Jace, what happened to that?"

I could break. I could tell her I've been having a hard time looking at myself in the mirror since the abortion. I could apologize for making her feel like I wasn't there for her. I could explain to her that I wish we were in a situation where we could've kept it. What I encouraged is a sin. This could be the moment that we end all the animosity. This isn't that moment. She doesn't understand where I'm coming from.

I swallow my emotion, and as cold as ice, I say, "I don't know, Belle. I just woke up one day and didn't love you anymore."

She throws the bag of candy on the floor and grabs the handle to leave.

"So that's it you're giving up?"

"You gave up the second you let those lies come out of your mouth. I can't do this. I can't talk to you." She steps out, and before slamming the door, she looks me in the eyes. "This broke me, Jace."

What does she expect? I have to come up with thousands of dollars in the next couple of weeks and have no fucking clue where to start. I do love you, Belle, but you're making it hard to. She's so obsessed with that fucking abortion she can't even have a regular conversation with me. I speed out of the parking lot before I can look at her again. My tires skid loud enough for her to hear. I know she's crying. I know she's frustrated with me, but I don't care. I'm just as frustrated with her.

All these damn girls are the same. I'm not surprised she brought up the money. That's all she cares about. Her saying all she wanted was support is bullshit. All she ever wanted was my hard-earned money. This whole thing has turned into one big fucked up mess. I want to get back to where we were. To be able to go to sleep in her arms and feel her magical fingers scratch my back. That would make this all go away. I have to make her see that.

CHAPTER THIRTY-SIX
Marabelle

"It's showtime!" Tabitha squeaks. She's next to me, adding final touches to her hair and makeup. "I can't believe this is my last play. I'm going to be a wreck tonight."

"Make sure you put on waterproof mascara," I interject. "I did, and I'm not even sure why. I didn't think I would be this emotional today. This is my first and last play."

Tabitha looks over at me. "Yeah, the drama club will make you mushy. I know we got off on the wrong foot, Belle, but you are very talented. I'm happy we get to do this together tonight."

"Me too, we weirdly work well together. I think the play saved my life this year," I awkwardly giggle. "Not to be dramatic or anything."

We burst into laughter together.

Eli stands behind my chair and looks at me through the mirror. "What are you two so giggly about?"

"Wow, Eli, you look hot!" Tabitha exclaims. "You really do, this costume with that hair," I pause for emphasis, "you look great. I'm so glad we both get to enjoy you on that stage."

"Oh yeah? Maybe we should make it an off-stage thing at the after-party tonight." He winks.

More laughter fills the space as we have grown to talk to each other in this nature. Joining the play has offered me a whole new perspective on what friendship means.

"No, but for real, I was just telling Belle how proud the theater nerds are of her to have adopted her in." Tabitha stands. "I'm going to warm up my vocals. I'll see you gorgeous souls out there."

Eli places both his hands on my shoulders. "How are you feeling?"

"I'm okay. A little nervous, but not as bad as I thought I would be."

"Good. That's good. If you start to panic out there, look at me. Most of our scenes are together, so remember it's me and you out there, no one else."

"Thank you."

"Thirty minutes to show time!" Ian shouts to the cast.

"Anyone special coming tonight?" I ask Eli.

"Just my mom and aunt, my dad thinks this shit is gay. You?"

"My whole family and my whole friend group," I bring the palm of my hand to slap my forehead.

"Lots of eyes on you. I know this is a stretch, but do you think Jace will come? You did say he was home for Spring break."

After the other night, I feel so uneasy about Jace. It was relieving to see him. I wanted to melt into him. I did melt into him. I let myself feel his touch, and it felt so good. Once I realized what I was doing, I snapped. It's like I can't be around him for too long because then I remember what he did to me.

"No shot. He doesn't even know I'm in the play this year."

"Well, if he lives in town, he had to have seen the millions of signs promoting it."

I didn't even think about that. Tabitha's and I's names are only on one digital sign outside the high school. Jace lives by me on the other side of town, so he definitely didn't see it.

"Jace doesn't care about shit like this. Even if he saw it, he wouldn't come," I emphasize.

"Your words are convincing me, Belle, but your eyes are saying something completely different."

I stand from my seat facing Eli. "Shut up, I don't want to think about this."

I feel my consciousness slipping from my body. I need my conscience fully present to be at my best tonight. You can't act without being inside your body. My oscillation of dissociation needs to reel itself back in. I need to be here. I need to do this for myself.

"I didn't mean to." Eli grabs my hands. "Let's shake it out."

We begin to wiggle and waggle our bodies from head to toe. It's a technique Mrs. Welsh taught us to manage our nerves.

"Fifteen minutes!" Ian shouts louder.

I run to the mirror before me, tucking my hair behind my unfamiliar ears. Tabitha runs to stand behind me. "Look at me!" My voice shakes.

"I know. We seem to be inside each other."

"I'm old!" I scream, rubbing my hands down the side of my face.

"I beg your pardon," Tabitha pouts.

"Oh, I'm like the crypt keeper!"

"Okay, that's enough."

The audience unites in a laugh. Everyone seems to be loving us so far.

Tabitha and I turn to face each other and scream in confusion.

"Ahhh, I want my body back," I shout.

I want my body back.

Will my body ever rejoin my mind? Have I broken the trust so far between the two that the convergence will never align?

The curtain closes.

Tabitha has her first solo song, and then Eli joins her for his second scene on stage as Jake.

"Excellent job, Belle, the people are loving you." Mrs. Welsh squeezes me on the shoulder.

I'm brought back into the present day. We're switching scenes, the first act has concluded.

Eli brushes me in passing, "Hey, you good?"

"Yeah, yeah, I'm fine. Good luck," I say, almost sounding like a question. I hug him. I don't usually hug; I'm not typically a hugger, but right now, I need one.

My solo is coming up soon, I have to change quickly and let the costume crew touch up my makeup. I bring myself into the back room, the room everyone competed for at the impostor party.

It's huge, basically half a classroom with freshly painted white walls. The left wall is lined with real director's chairs, and the right side is divided by pop-up changing rooms. There's even a separate bathroom in here. After the party, Ian decided that we could all share the room. It's never been done before because whoever wins the game is typically too selfish to make that sacrifice.

I let the girls press extra powder into my face so I'm not shining on stage. Ian is operating tonight. I really didn't understand the significance of his role until dress rehearsal. He's calling the shots, directing everyone where they need to be. He's sort of the glue of this whole operation.

"Marabelle, we need Marabelle to center stage in 30 seconds!" Ian's voice echoes in the hall. Holding the edge of the door frame, he peaks his head into the state-of-the-art dressing room. "Marabelle, there you are," he says relieved. "Let's go girl."

"Coming, coming," I say, taking a quick look in the mirror and running my hands through my hair.

We start to rush to the stage together. "Your solo is up after this. Are you ready?"

"I think so," I half smile.

"You look beautiful. You sound even better. You're going to kill it."

"Thank you, Ian."

"Okay, stand here, and when the curtain closes, take your stage."

I exhale, "okay."

"Oh, and Belle.."

"Yeah?"

"My brother is here. I'm sure he's particularly excited for this number." Ian winks and disappears. The curtain closes, and I take the stage.

His brother.

His stepbrother.

Nick.

Nick is here.

The curtain draws open, and the warm stage lights accompany me. They remind me of the lights I burned my eyes into in the abortion clinic. There's nowhere to look, nowhere to turn. You either look at the monitor alongside Light Blue Scrubs or you sear your corneas on the fluorescent overhead lighting.

Pretend it's the sun, Marabelle.

Warm, beautiful sun rays bless my body with kindness. I sing and forget every single thought that perpetuates through my mind. I'm a little girl again. Setting up my living room to perform for my Mommy. This microphone was born to be in my hand. This is the song I struggled most with throughout the year. Mrs. Welsh wrote it to accompany how Tess Coleman feels inside her daughter's body. Every rehearsal and every time I looked at my mom, I heard this song. It was hard for me to make it come to life with my voice because it was all so personal to me.

There were moments I fantasized about having a Freaky Friday of my own. Switch places with someone else; maybe they would understand what I feel like in my skin now. What it felt like to tell the person you love you're pregnant. What it felt to lose that much blood. To live with this much uncertainty. I think uncertainty is what will lead me to insanity. I'm still waiting for someone to understand.

I hit the last note with ease and the crowd roars in applause. Being on stage is like a double mirror. You can't really see out because of the blinding lights, but the audience can see in. It makes me feel safer that way. I don't want to see their reactions or who's sitting where. It would be too distracting. All I need to know is their validation through sound. I follow that sound, letting it guide me through the night.

It's the intermission. The audience has broken for snacks and bathroom time. The main cast is lined up in those chairs, fixing hair and makeup and taking a moment to catch their breath. It's absolute chaos in here. Who's bumping into who, who needs water, who's complaining about their shitty vocals. It's hard to focus on one thing. I've never been a part of this environment before. My body is being hit with these bumps of adrenaline to keep me going. This feeling is addicting. It's exciting and nerve-racking, and I love it here. I need to pee before we have to take our places again. The line in here is way too long, so I'm going to sneak into the halls and go upstairs.

"Eli, I'm going to pee upstairs. Do you want to come?" I smile at him with pleading eyes.

"Ah, sure. But let's use the one in the home EC room. No one will be there."

We link arms and make our escape. Eli has started to feel like a best friend to me in a different way than Brandon and Joey. Brandon and Joey know the Marabelle, who likes to party, the girl who always has a smile on her face, bringing everyone else up. I've shared deeper feelings with them through the years, but in all honesty, we don't spend much time together sober. They know me as Marabelle before the abortion. Eli knows me as the girl after.

"I'm so proud of you," he hugs my arm closer to him.

"Awe, you're adorable." We take each step in two. His long legs guide us.

"No, seriously, Belle. I know how hard this year has been for you. I'm really happy you didn't quit the play. You're stronger than you give yourself credit for."

We pause before splitting ways into our designated gendered rooms. "Thank you, but I put on a brave face."

We both use the bathroom, not bullshitting too much as we walk back to the stage. We can hear the crowd of people grabbing their last-minute snacks and finding their seats before we begin again.

CHAPTER THIRTY-SEVEN

There are moments when I feel like the abortion never happened. Like that was a whole separate entity from my being.

It happened two months ago. My entire world was flipped upside down, and I was left with the right to choose. My frustration with Jace is all rooted in hurt. Planted, watered, and sprouted into an agonizing feeling inside my gut. It's unfathomable to process how he acted through the entire thing.

Do you love me?

Yes.

Then, nothing else matters.

What happened to those words? Nothing else matters in the context of our petty fights. Jace had no idea what was to come. I had no idea what was happening inside my own body. He shouldn't have said that. I shouldn't have let him say that.

My mind does this thing where it flashes memories and moments between us. It's like it reminds me of why I love him and how I've grown to hate him. The hating him part is so much fuzzier than the loving him part. I try to reason with my mind, begging for it to show me more of the bad. I try to understand how he was feeling when I was pregnant, but every time I do, I'm left with the hurt that his curiosity wasn't deep enough to ask me. I want so badly to know how he feels. When I saw him the other night, something behind his eyes was pained. It pissed me off because how could he be in more pain than me?

I break out of my reflection frame. There are a couple of scenes left. Do not lose it now, Marabelle.

He's not here.

"Belle, this is it," Mrs. Welsh comes to stand to my left.

Tabitha comes to stand to my right. "Let's fucking rock this!"

And that's exactly what we do. This is my favorite scene. I have to play guitar for Tabitha backstage to rescue her while she figures out how to fake rock out on stage.

We're fucking killing it. Having the most fun we could possibly have on a stage. This beats any party, any shot of vodka. Any boy I've ever kissed for entertainment or weed I've smoked to numb. This is feeling. My heart pounds with the sound of rhythmic claps that join us in. These kinds of moments you don't get in rehearsal. Having an auditorium packed with people cheering for you is indescribable. I look at Tabitha, and she looks at me; we make the perfect peanut butter and jelly.

I join her in singing the last verse.

Don't wanna grow up. I wanna get out. Hey, take me away. I want to shout out. Take me away, away. Away, away, away...

For the first time, I don't want to get out. I don't want to be taken away. I want to be right here inside my body, inside my mind, feeling every single thing this moment has to offer me.

Round and round, here we go again. Same old

story, the same old end. Turn my head and turn back again. Same old stuff never ends.

I have to stop the cycle.

I close my eyes. The audience applauds.

I make a silent apology in my head to myself: I'm sorry I did this to you body, it was nice to feel us united tonight, even if it was just for a little bit.

CHAPTER THIRTY-EIGHT

Hugs, tears, and praise is all that takes place once the final curtain closes. They gave the seniors extra recognition for our final bow. I thought I would feel unworthy to be out there with them. They have all been doing this for so much longer than I have. I felt anything but that. Standing out there hand in hand with my cast mates was so moving. I even cried. These people are my friends, and I am a proud theater nerd.

"Marabelle! Over here!" Lindsay waves her hand in the air. I run to my sister wrapping my arms around her and picking her up into a hug. My body is coated in chills.

"Belle's, that was incredible. You were incredible!" My Mom wipes her tears.

"Whoo, I got to catch my breath," I place my hand on my chest. The hallways are flooded with friends, family, and flowers.

My Dad hands me a bouquet of flowers and kisses my forehead, "You are a star, my Belle's."

Affection with my Dad is few and far between; I lean into him, enjoying what he offers me. "Thank you."

"Total slay, Belle."

"Yeah, seriously, you would have thought you've been doing this for years," Lindsay's dance friends compliment me.

I feel showered in love. I *feel*.

We stand around doing some mingling. I introduced my parents to Mrs. Welsh. Everyone is in high spirits, so all the introductions are going great. Mrs. Welsh thinks my sister is a real hoot and is already trying to recruit her into the drama club when she enters high school. She said if she's my sister, she'll be a natural.

Eli skips over to the corner my family is occupying. He bows his head to all of them in greeting, "Hello, Alvarez family. I'm Eli. Marabelle's best friend."

"Nice to finally meet you, Eli," my mom shakes his hand and eyes me like she understands what's going on between us. I shake my head with attitude because that's disgusting. Eli, seriously, is my best friend.

"Well, now I know where Belle gets her looks. It's a pleasure to meet you." Eli will always flirt with anything that has a pulse, including my Mother.

"Belle, we're all going back to Ian's for the after-party. He said for everyone to change and show up whenever."

"Ians?"

"Yes, Ians." His eyes grow with reassurance. "It'll be fine. I'll meet you there?"

"Yeah, let's meet there. I still have to find my friends, change, and all that."

"Okay, darling. I'll see you in a bit. It's nice to meet all of you!" He waves goodbye to my family.

I decided to head home with my friends. They were so excited to see me after that I couldn't get enough of it. My mom had packed me a bag because she had a feeling I would want to get to the after-party as fast as possible. I waited around, hoping to see Nick. He never appeared. I don't know why I thought he would be waiting there to congratulate me. We're all packed into Brandon's car, going over the highlights of the night.

"Belle, I never thought acting could be cool, but you made it look cool," Joey shouts from the back seat.

"I didn't think it could be cool either," I laugh. It's so fun, though, being on stage like that. I can't even describe it. I was having a great time."

"We were having a great time watching!" Elena emphasizes.

"So you're all going to come with me to the after-party, right?" I ask.

Brandon turns down the music to say, "Yeah, unless it's just the cast, then we probably shouldn't intrude."

"No, no, it's def like everyone. Ian said to us to invite whoever you want." I add.
"Cool, I'm excited. I really liked them last time we all partied together," Kelly says.

"Take a right here, Brandon," Madison interrupts. "We're going to Elena's to get ready."

"Roger that," Brandon salutes the air, and all of our bodies sway to the left, responding to his sharp turn.

Why are we going to Elena's? I thought we were going to Kelly's to get ready since we keep all the alcohol there. "Why are we going to Elena's?" I don't let my tone cut too deep.

"Well, because her house is closest to Ian's, so we can walk over," Madison replies matter-of-factly.

I wish Madison would choke on her words and die.

That was dark. I can't believe my brain went there. I know why it did, but I didn't know it could get that dark. I shake it off and respond nonchalantly. "Okay, as long as I can get a drink in me as soon as possible!"

CHAPTER THIRTY-NINE

I squat on the toilet, mesmerized by the pattern surrounding me. The purple daisies on the wall seem so vibrant now. I never noticed them like that. I've been sitting on the toilet so long everyone is going to think my pee turned into a poo. It didn't. I haven't been in here since I peed on a stick, forever altering me.

I want to burn this room to the ground. I want every fiber of material to go up in flames, taking its memory with it. Do objects hold memories? Do the walls recognize me? I place my right hand on the bump my belly forms when I sit down. I hold it there and accompany it by the left one. Overlapped with one another, I glance down at my hands, holding what is no longer there.

You're a fool. A dramatic fool, Belle. It's not that serious.

"Marabelle!" There are three knocks at the door. "Let's get this show on the road. We have three shots waiting for you." Joey's muffled voice sounds through the door.

"Coming!" I flush frantically.

Snap the fuck out of it. Tonight is going to be a good night.

It was three shots down the hatch, some pictures crammed into Elena's mirror, and we're off. My friends continue to remind me that tonight is for me, and I can't deny it feels good.

The music is pumping as soon as we enter the familiar space. The last time I walked in here, I had no idea what was ahead of me. Tonight, I think I have a better idea.

"Ahhhhh, there we are! Now we have both co-stars in attendance!" Ian brings me into a half-hug. "Please, please help yourselves. We have tons of liquor in the kitchen. What's mine is yours." He gestures, encouraging all my friends to go get drunk.

"Ian, I've been wanting to ask you for a while," I pause, "Why don't you want to be on stage?"

"That's the thing. I do want to be on stage, I'm the most dramatic person I know."

I nod in agreeance.

"But every time I've tried, my nerves get the best of me. I learned very quickly I'm better off behind the stage bossing people around. It takes a strong person to get up there and do what you did tonight." He booty bumps me.

I smile. "Can I get you a drink?"

"I'm okay, darling. I see someone I need to go flirt with!"

"Okay," I laugh, and he's already stalked off before I can finish.

Another party, another drunk night. We take shots, we dance, we take more shots, we crack up, we pour ourselves a mixie, and people start to break off in normal party fashion. My mind's space has ceased all responsibilities and worries, and the only thing I can focus on is Nick. He has to be here. I want him so badly to be here.

I make my way to the sliding back door. The warm Spring air snakes up the length of my bare legs. The tiny shed has the same hue of light illuminating through the window. I know who turned on that light. Following the same path that led me here months ago, I open the shed door and walk inside.

Nicholas Ricci is sitting on the makeshift couch. The brunette with the bob is right next to him. Nick's head whips up, looking me dead in the eyes.

"Belle."

"Nick." I tilt my head towards the bob.

I don't want to know her name. She doesn't deserve a name. She's the brunette Nick was with at the other party. She is just brunette, she is just bob. Please don't introduce her Nick, please don't give her any significance to your life.

She sucks down her vape and blows the smoke perpendicular to her face. "I'm Janelle."

She thinks she has power over me. She thinks sitting there next to him means she has the upper hand. Silly girl.

I spread my legs positioning the upside-down bucket between them. I sit a foot away from Nick, three feet from the brunette. This has to be strategic. My mind computes the situation in nanoseconds.

"We were about to smoke. Would you like to join?" Nick grabs the joint from behind his ear. God, I forgot how sexy he is.

"Sure, if you guys don't mind." I turn to face her.

Janelle looks at Nick, waiting for him to retract his offer. The pause is too long. She has to say something. "Not at all," she says with a sarcastic smirk.

Nick lights the joint and passes it to her first. He's not going to make this easy for me. I respect him for that. Whoever you pass the joint to first sends a message. It's basic smoking etiquette.

"Did you guys come to the play tonight? Or have you been here the whole time?" When I ask deliberate questions, I like to give two options. It forces the person to pick one, cueing the conversation to flow in my favor.

"I was at the play," Nick says.

"I don't go to Titan and don't care about some silly little play."

"Then why are you here?" This comes out aggressive, more aggressive than I intended. I feel the need to defend my people. "This is the plays after party so why wouldn't you go to a party in your own town?"

She chuckles to herself. No one else is laughing. "I came to keep Nick company." She bumps his shoulder, attempting to be playful.

"I see," my eyes bounce back and forth between the two of them. "I didn't know you were incapable of being alone Nick."

He half smiles, trying not to entertain what is clearly happening in front of him. He has to be enjoying this. My phone vibrates in my back pocket. I grab it to check.

Madison: Where are you? I need to ask you something !?!

Whatever Madison needs to ask me can wait. It's probably some stupid question about one of the boys she wants to hook up with.

I lock my phone, rejoining the two in front of me.

"Need to go somewhere?" Brunette articulates.

"No, I'm good." I'm done playing this game. This isn't about this useless girl. This is about

Nick and I. I don't want to fall for this petty shit. I know what I came in here for.

I hand the joint back to Nick leaning close to his face. "Can we talk? Alone?"

He has every right to shut me out. I shut things down between the two of us. It was because of Jace. At least, that's what I told him, that I had a particular asshole in my life that I was still dealing with. That was only 59% true. The other 41% was that I was fucking pregnant and scared shitless. That's a real boner killer to a potentially new relationship.

My eyes are begging as they look into his. Please don't shut me out, Nick. I know you see something in me. I think I might be starting to see something in myself. Jace isn't good for me; he never has been, but you, Nick, are good for me. If I let myself fall for you, maybe I'll never look back at Jace. Please, Nick, merely take a fraction of my measly pain away.

"Janelle, would you mind leaving us alone for a minute?" Nick readjusts in his seat.

She nurses the vape again, "You've got to be kidding."

When he doesn't respond, she stands abruptly. Angry and humiliated by Nick's submission to me, she kicks the bucket on my left to make room for her exit. "Whatever. You're both pathetic!" She slams the door and leaves.

"Have we switched roles, Nicholas Ricci?"

"What do you mean?" He says, finally relaxing his shoulders.

"Shitty men," I say, motioning my hands in an imaginary scale, "or shitty women," and I shoot the hand symbolizing women above my head. My tight white long sleeve comes up with me revealing more of my stomach than I intended. Nick's eyes drop to my body, scanning the exposed skin with a deep stare.

My core tightens from the graze of his eyes. I feel the blush form in my cheeks, trying not to let my giddiness show.

"Marabelle, she is nothing to me."

"Then why was she here with you? And why were you escorting her down the stairs at the senior class party?" The second part slips. I didn't want him to know that I had seen them before. I no longer hold the upper hand.

"She's one of my buddies' sisters, Will." He smiles at me. "I didn't want to go to the senior party because none of my friends would be there, but she convinced me to go. Told me I would regret it if I didn't. She said she would come with me so I had somebody. She's flirty, and I won't lie, I'm a bit flirty back, but we've never kissed or done anything."

His immediate explanation is too kind. I would have had to rip the words out of Jace's mouth to get him to confess even a tiny piece of my accusations. Nick reassures me, even when I don't deserve it.

"Even if I did kiss her," his tone becomes playful, "it would never compare to you."

"So you've been thinking about us kissing?" I bite my tongue. "Because I have been thinking about it a lot."

"Yeah," his voice drags, "you've been occupying a lot of my brain space, considering I don't see you much."

That's my fault, I did this.

He switches the subject when he sees my mind spiraling, "You were amazing tonight. I was cheering for you so loud the people next to me definitely thought I was obsessed with you."

"I wouldn't mind if you were obsessed with me, Nick," I drop my gaze, flirting with my eyes.

He shakes his head with the biggest smile on his face. It's beyond contradicting. "I tried to find you after but got caught up with my family." Hew confesses.

"I tried to find you after, too. And I really tried not to think about you during."

My phone vibrates in my back pocket again. I ignore it.

I place my hand on Nick's thigh, right above his knee. My body is longing to make contact with him. "I'm sorry about the last time we spoke. I was going through a lot and didn't know how to tell you that." That's the most honest thing that has come out of my mouth all year. I take a breath, "I'm getting it together. I want to get it together for myself."

But mostly for you.

He places his hand over mine. It sends serotonin to my brain. "I don't need you to be perfect, Belle. I just can't play all these games with you. I don't think I've actually ever said it, but I like you, Belle."

"I like you too, Nick. It's hard for me to let people in, but I want to let you in."

Our undeniable physical attraction is what first drove me to Nick. When I submitted to him in this shed a couple of months ago, I was willing to let him use me. I had very little respect for myself and my body.

He tucks my hair behind my ear. He drags one piece through his fingertips and twirls it around in a loop. "I like your curly hair."

"Do I look ugly with it straight?" I tease.

"Not at all, but you look more Belle like this," he slides his thumb to the swell of my bottom lip. "You look more, Marabelle, with it natural."

This man strikes a cord deep inside my psyche. He hits the spots of Marabelle that I have worked so hard to bury. She's happy to be coming back to the surface. She's been drowning for so long.

I kiss him. It's delicate and intimate. His hands hold either side of my face and steady me from the force of his lips. Our faces remain connected as he explores my mouth with that godforsaken tongue. His hands give me security, and I let myself soften into him.

He breaks the kiss slowly, still keeping both hands on me. "I've been thinking about that kiss for too fucking long." He brings me in again, savoring each moment our lips and tongues connect.

A hushed moan escapes me. Everything is perfect. The play was phenomenal. The liquor in me is keeping my blood warm. Nick kissing me is just the cherry on top of my perfect night. I could stay like this for hours. I could be with him forever.

Is Nick my forever?

Footsteps jolt our attention to the shed door. I turn around, preparing myself for Janelle to walk through this stupid door. Nick is thinking the same. He grabs me by either side of my thighs, lifting me into his lap. I straddle his waist, surprised by his sudden strength.

"I don't care who's coming through that door. I wasn't done."

He swallows my giggle with another kiss. I like that he isn't ashamed to be with me. I like that if it's Janelle, he's sending a very clear message to her.

The door flies open.

"Belle."

CHAPTER FORTY

"Ah, hi, so sorry. I didn't mean to interrupt," Elena says, closing the door behind her. "But I need Belle."

Nick and I look at each other, confused by the uneasiness in her voice and annoyed that she is interrupting a very sacred moment we've been longing for.

"Can't it wait? We're obviously in the middle of something," I rebuttal.

"Yeah, it can't unless you want this to end badly," she motions between Nick and me.

I have no idea what she's talking about. This is ending badly because of her. Why is she doing this to me? Why is she taking my one moment of happiness away?

Elena continues, "Belle, trust me, I wouldn't be doing this if I wasn't your best friend."

Nick grabs my hips. "You should go. It sounds like a friend emergency. I'll meet you after, I promise."

He lowers his voice so only I can hear him. He whispers in my ear, sending chills down my whole spine. I love that he still doesn't care who's watching. "I'm still not done with you."

The smile that forms on my face is warm and fuzzy. "Alright, I'm coming, I'm coming." I get off of Nick, bending down once more to kiss him on the cheek. We've gone from struggling situation ship to public displays of affection real quick.

Elena reaches for my hand and drags me out of the shed, slamming the door shut. "Jeez, Elena, ease up. What the fuck is going on."

"Did you not look at any of Madison's texts?"

"I saw the first one, but no. I was busy," I shout, motioning towards the shed behind us.

"Jace called her."

Those three words eject me so far from my body. Elena is talking and explaining, and all I can hear is the hum of her voice.

He's not here.

Oh yes, he is. I told myself he wasn't here all night. I told myself that even if he saw the hundreds of signs around town, there was no way he would come to a stupid nerdy play. Jace hates that shit. That's what I told Eli. He hates it. Why would he come? Did he come for me? Did he watch every minute of my performance? Did he like it?

"Belle! Are you even listening to me?" She shouts.

Now I understand Elena's urgency. Her protection makes sense. "I-I. I didn't hear a word you said."

"Apparently, Madison saw him during the intermission, and she assumed you guys were back together. She didn't mention it until he texted her when we got here. He asked if it was cool for him to come. That's when she texted you to make sure it was okay. I honestly assumed you said yes because I didn't hear otherwise from

Madison. I kept drinking, forgot about it, and you were nowhere to be found. I didn't think twice because these are your people now, and everyone wants to talk to you tonight."

"So at what point did Jace get here, and you realize I didn't give the okay?"

"Well, I asked Madison a little while ago, and she said you never answered, that she texted you twice. And then I thought Madison's stupid ass didn't realize if you guys were back together, then Jace wouldn't be asking her if it was cool for him to come to the party; he would just come even if he was making sure it wasn't closed invite. He tricked her. "

I close my eyes and take a very deep breath. I hate Madison. I hate Elena. I hate her purple daisy-covered bathroom. What fucking idiots. How didn't she realize immediately that Madison's a moron?

"He's looking for you. I thought it was a good idea for me to find you before he saw you straddling another dude."

"I fucking hate this."

"I know Belle, but—"

I cut her off. "Please. Don't. Do not pretend like you know even a bit of how I feel."

"I try to," her voice grows strong, "but you don't tell me shit anymore. I don't even know where you and Jace stand after what happened, but I figured you didn't want him to see you like *that*."

I appreciate her coming to get me. I really do, but her tone is all over the place with me. She's right, I don't tell her shit anymore. It's hard for her to understand. She makes a lot of jokes about the abortion. They seem light-hearted and rooted in good intentions, I think, but it bothers me. I was affected by those insignificant jokes. Before the abortion, I would've been the first to crack them. Naive and unaware that my words could hurt someone. Now, my own words are hurting me. I told her to stop, never to bring it up again, that I don't think about it, so she shouldn't either.

Lies, lies, and more lies. There's nothing that consumes my mind more than the abortion. I told her to stop, but I was really screaming at her for help.

"I need a fucking drink, I can't do this right now!" I shout and stalk off.

I'm so close to breaking. I want someone to hurt. I want to hurt someone with my words. Cut so deep it leaves a mark. This treacherous vodka cannot get into my bloodstream fast enough. I shouldn't have to wait for this alcohol to kick in. It should be immediate.

I shouldn't have had to wait.

OH MY GOD, enough already! I'm pissed off and beyond irritated that my friends can't have my back just this once. I chug and refill and chug and refill.

As I refill my third cup something in the atmosphere around me heightens.

I become aware of what's happening around me. I feel the air change and my body tense. I respond to his presence every time. I am the Earth surrendering to his gravity. A hand comes to the small of my back—his hand. He presses into me from behind. I close my eyes, enjoying whatever touch we have left.

We don't speak. We both stay like that for a moment, reminiscing on what our magnificent touch does to both of us.

"Hi," he says, still glued to the back of me.

"Hi."

"How are you?" He asks.

"I'm good," somehow much better now. "How are you?"

"I am well. Do you want to go somewhere quieter?"

I keep my eyes focused in front of me. We're in the center of the kitchen, surrounded by too many drunk teenagers. I lock eyes with Eli from across the room. He's never even seen Jace before, but from the look in his eyes, I know, he knows, this is him. I give him a nod that I'm okay. I shake my head to answer Jace's question.

I don't let myself think. He takes my hand, guiding me through the crowd to the outside. Our rhythm right back on beat.

We reach the front yard. He takes a seat on one of the porch chairs.

His legs spread open, and he leans his chest back. Insufferably relaxed, his energy radiates confidence. He has this. He knows that.

"Why are you here, Jace?" I ask, unintentionally drawing closer to him.

"I came to your play. I had no idea you were doing any of that."

He doesn't ask me why I never told him, and I take note of that. If he had, the conversation would have plummeted. He doesn't want to go down that road. He wants to keep me on his side.

He runs his hands through his hair. It got longer, much longer. I didn't notice last time because he kept his hood puffed up, covering most of it. He looks so handsome tonight. So alluring. He's got his favorite green flannel on and some thick black jeans. I missed his siren blue eyes. I miss the way they scan me. My brain keeps him on a pedestal, the length to the top blurry and irrelevant.

He continues, "You were fucking awesome. I always knew you could sing from little snippets in the car, but never like that. That was badass."

He knows his words feel good. I smile.

"I'm really proud of you." I never thought I could hear those words out of Jace's mouth. I told myself never to expect them because that's not who Jace is. "*Freaky Friday's* your favorite movie, right?" He asks.

"Yeah, one of them."

"Yeah, I remember you telling me that," he laughs. "Cool to see it as a play."

"Our director is a genius, she rewrote the whole thing."

"Very interesting," his eyes scan my body. "Can you come here for a second?" He motions his two fingers in.

I go to him.

He takes a piece of my hair closest to my face and runs it between his fingers. I look down at him.

"Your hair has been straight the last two times I saw you."

"Well, you only saw me 2 nights ago, Jace," I tease.

"You had to have it like this for the play?"

"Mmmhh." Now that we're standing so close the smell of him consumes me. I know that scent. It's all too familiar. Blindfold me, put me in an isolated room. Take away all my other senses. I would be able to point out Jace's scent every single time. It's fresh. It's intoxicating. It's uniquely him.

"It's nice like this." He looks me in my eyes and drops the piece.

There's this bubbling urge inside me begging to be released. I want to talk about it. I need to know how you feel about it. If we go down that road, we never come out. I tried to the other night, and he spit lies in my face. I always want to ruin our good moments because they're murky from the bad ones.

It feels so good to be good with you, Jace.

Choke it down, Marabelle. Savor what he's presenting you right now. Let's not talk about it. I'm responding to what my body likes. I will look no further than that.

"I can't believe you texted Madison, of all people," I say playfully.

"She's always flirting with everyone she shouldn't be. I knew it would be an easy in for me." He shrugs. "She obliged perfectly."

"Yeah, I know she's an idiot," the words slip like butter. They're mean.

"Doesn't matter now because it got me here," he slides the palm of his hand into my back pocket, scooping me in between his legs.

"Jace, I—"

Before I finish, our lips collide. Positive and negative. My resistant spine immediately falls into his hold. The promise I made to myself evaporating. There is no stopping the cycle. It's desperate and passionate. Everything inside me has lit on fire. Our tongues lap over one another in our preferred manner. I hurry to grab either side of his face, pushing into him further. My hands fit perfectly in the crevice of his cheeks.

We pause at the exact same time. Breathing, heaving, but not moving. He looks into my eyes, and I fall. I kiss him again. We scramble in each other's hold, leaving no room for the memories to kick in.

His grip on my ass grows ravenous. He's greedy with his touch. Rough and loving. His motions are wild and consuming. I want him to tear my clothes off. We moan into each other's mouths, so caught up in the moment.

He breaks the kiss suddenly, reaching under my shirt to feel my flesh under his hands. He snakes his hands down the length of my body, landing back in his favorite place.

I peck him once more quickly and murmur, "I missed you." The words effortlessly spill.

He nods his head once. "Me too."

I can feel his emotion inside my heart, and I know his words are genuine. The way he kissed me was layered with a million "I miss you" s.

A grin paints his soft face. "What do you say we get out of here so I can kiss you properly? I don't need to be making out with you outside of a party like I'm still in high school."

"I am still in high school," I roll my eyes.

"Yeah, but I'm not," he jokes, "Besides, your spot in my bed has been waiting for you."

Just like that, he sings my favorite song. There's no room for logic. "Did you drive?"

"Yeah."

I turn around to look behind me remembering that other people occupy this planet. "Um, do you mind if I meet you there? This is a play celebration, and I haven't done much celebrating with my cast." He doesn't like my request. I struggle for wording so that he grants me permission. "Give me one hour. Just to have one more drink and say goodbye."

What am I going to do about Nick?

He stands, looking down at me. "That's fine, text me when you're on your way." He kisses me once more, reassuring our agreement. There's something different about this kiss. Some essence of finality infused through it.

CHAPTER FORTY-ONE

I skip back to the house, rejoining the party. Each step brings me further and further away from my happiness. My body and mind are merging to take control. There is no more pushing it down. It's up, ready to unleash.

I don't know what just happened. Am I an idiot, or did I make the right decision? That all happened fast. It felt like I was home. It was like nothing had happened, and all the pieces fit right back into place. We kissed. I mean, he kissed me. Hot, passionate, face grabbing, neck holding, kissing. That is exactly what I missed.

There were moments we paused and soaked in the silence of each other's company. Like all of this was meant to be. I want to cry, but I want to smile. I told him one hour. Can I really do that?

I don't know if it's the fumes from the party or my logic rejoining my brain, but all I can think about is Nick. My logic loves to question my intuition. My half-sex with Nick was obviously better, but the love that's still there with Jace is too strong. I wonder what he's thinking about. I wish this could go somewhere. But I was pregnant, and he showed his true colors. And now I'm here sneaking out of the party that's supposed to be celebrating me to go to somebody I used to know. Someone needs to yell at me. I don't know what this means for me, but all I know is that being cuddled up with him in my spot in his bed is a place I want to be in for the rest of my life.

He is my home. But I'm trying to figure out if I can stay in the house when the walls catch fire. I lit the match. I did it. I flipped that pregnancy test over, changing everything forever. I take responsibility for my actions, but you still haven't. Loan me an apology. Tell me you're sorry for the way you treated me. Tell me that this was all too hard for you, and you didn't know how to handle it. Tell me you realize now what it was like for me. Please empathize with the pain I carry every single day after. I may have lit the match, Jace, but you fueled the fire.

Every wall,

every memory,

being scorched in its path.

There's one room left to be burned. I'm holding onto every piece of it. My lungs are full of smoke. I'm suffering. Can't you see I'm suffering, Jace?

Nick stands across from me at the island in the kitchen. He waited for me—that whole time. The whole time, I made out with Jace.

We make eye contact. The salty water pooling in my eyes overflows. My tears fall simultaneously in two parallel lines, racing to the finish line as they fall off my cheeks. I do nothing to stop them. He's confused by my vulnerability, but he's not scared.

I'm scared, TERRIFIED. I'm still lying on parchment in the cold, cold clinic. Being asked if I'm sure I want to do this. I'm still curled up in fetal position, screaming in agony as my body releases copious amounts of blood.

I don't know if I can move forward with you, Nick, because my body feels like it's never coming out of the past.

Epilogue
8 months later...

The air is starting to get cold again. I finally caved in and threw on a jacket over my hoodie today. I hate this time of year—right before all the holidays, right before we have to oblige to daylight savings time.

I got a hot coffee today. They made it perfectly. Light and sweet, exactly how I like it. I finished up my coffee date with Elena and we went our separate ways to class. All of our friends are coming to visit us this weekend, so we were deciding who would sleep where.

We never planned on applying to the same school. It sort of happened that way. I'm really happy it did. It's working out great for us. We decided if we were going to go to college together it was important for us not to room together. We obviously are still best friends, but we didn't want to close ourselves off to meeting new people.

My roommate Jessica is great. We get along well. She's quite the opposite of me in many ways, but she gives me a good perspective on things. She's from Virginia, so we have some cultural differences, but we've taught each other a lot. She tells me my Jersey accent is funny, but I'm still not fully convinced I have one. Jess has a strong sense of self. She believes in spirits, and energy, and shit like that.

We stay up at night talking about life. She loves to get all philosophical about things. In the beginning, it would annoy me. But now, when she speaks, I can secretly reason with her mind. She's so open about everything. It makes me more inclined to share.

Today, I have my midterm for my poetry class. My major is still undecided, but I'll have to make a decision soon. My decision-making process is still pretty clouded. College has given me the excuse to rebrand myself entirely.

You can be anyone in college. No one knows you here. They only know what you tell them besides your childhood best friend who came to college with you. I think it's for the best, though; Elena likes this version of me; she says I've changed a lot. It's hard for me to notice, but I feel lighter and maybe even nicer. It's even become a little more pleasant to live in my own mind. I am fully leaning into the version of me that resulted from the abortion.

We had to keep a journal for this class all year. Some prompts were given to us by the professor, but others were just from our own thoughts. It's been really healing for me. Expressing the words outside of how I feel them in my brain is magical. I've gone above and beyond for every assignment simply because it's helping me heal.

Our professor wants us to read one poem from our journal to the class for a midterm grade. I was up all night reading and rereading my journal. I waited until Jess fell asleep because I knew it would be hard for me to read back the words I'd written throughout the last couple of months. I cried a lot. It hurts to recognize how dark your thoughts can get. Reading everything through again just showed me how far I've come.

The way I wrote at the beginning of this semester was still chaotic. It was filled with anger and sadness, cascading into a hate spiral. You can see how I've eased up, where I have eased up, and the exact date when my words on paper went from a debilitating weight to lighter. It was the day I chose myself.

I wrote this poem last night. It was the conclusion of all my words.

"Marabelle." Professor Winston calls as we clap for my peer, walking back to her seat. Shit. I'm next. Inhale. Exhale.

I don't let the nerves get to me. I pretend I'm on stage again, and the lights serve as a double-sided mirror. I imagine it's the sun.

"When you're ready," the professor tilts his head.

I grip both sides of my sacred book. The edges worn from the countless uses.

"Forging meaning, building identity," I say.

I conjure up a little bit of my pain. I tap into it as I recite the poem aloud:

"For me, I knew the meaning as soon as I had went back. Same place. Same smell. Same attitudes about what had happened. I tried to get through to him. God, did I want him to understand. He didn't. And he never would. At least, never admit it to me. Same attitudes, same ego. I thought going back was the right thing to do, what needed to be done. He, as always, had a much different agenda. I turned my back to him. He asked me to face him. I knew in that moment if I turned around the cycle would keep repeating. I never turned again. I got in my car and left, finally getting it. The meaning was in the cycle. It needed to end in order for me to transcend. That's exactly what I did.

I became someone I didn't recognize, perhaps my authentic self. The version of me I was too scared to be with him. What we created never developed, but that wasn't the point of it. It was never supposed to develop. Never supposed to be ours. It was the key that unlocked me. Now, that doesn't take away from any of my grief or heartache. I am still grieving that development. He still loves to remind me what could've been, as I am painfully reminded that I took it away. I will forever be connected to him, but not by the meaning I once thought, rather, the meaning that found me.

Muscles tight, abdominals on the verge of shattering. Never, ever relaxed around him. My body was protecting what I could not see. Constantly holding my breath around the man I love, constantly…. My identity was birthed through the death of us.

All of us.

All three of us.

Forever

    my

        love

            forever

                my

                    baby."

Author Note

I can't even begin to process the journey it has taken me to get here. I wrote this story by accident. Fresh out of college, I moved to Costa Rica for a month and forgot how much I loved to write without constraints. I began writing again with no limits or consciousness of what I was creating. It was just fun.

After a couple of months of struggling to find my place in this world, I came back to this story. I am incredibly grateful for any of you who chose to take a chance on me all because I took a chance on myself.

I believe in this story and the power it holds in our world. My intention was to make you feel seen, heard, and empowered. I think we all have a piece of Marabelle in us. Abortion is not something you should feel ashamed of or embarrassed by. For me, I had to learn that by sharing this with you <3

Thank you for reading my words. Stay tuned for a whole lot more of them.

Yours truly,
Deanna Parisi

Where to find me (:

Made in the USA
Las Vegas, NV
21 January 2025